# CROSSING THE GAP

# Crossing the Gap

A NOVELIST'S ESSAYS

C. J. KOCH

Chatto & Windus

LONDON

Published in 1987 by
Chatto & Windus Ltd
40 William IV Street
London WC2N 4DF

British Library Cataloguing in Publication Data

Koch, C. J.
Crossing the gap: a novelist's essays.
I. Title
824   PR9619.3.K64

ISBN 0 7011 3216 7

'Maybe It's Because I'm a Londoner', composed by Hubert Gregg,
© 1947 by Francis Day & Hunter Ltd.
Reproduced by permission of Francis Day & Hunter Ltd, London,
and, for Australia and New Zealand,
J. Albert & Son Pty Ltd, Sydney.

Photoset by Rowland Phototypesetting Ltd
Bury St Edmunds, Suffolk
Printed in Great Britain by
Redwood Burn Ltd
Trowbridge, Wilts

# CONTENTS

# AUTHOR'S NOTE

Many of these essays began as talks; some began as book reviews. All have been considerably expanded, and a number have been amalgamated with other material when the marriage seemed happy.

Novelists and poets are bound to mimic in some way the pulse of the society that produced them: one that's unique, its rhythm never to be repeated. At a certain age, one realises that the pulse has changed; and this has provided the common theme of these essays, in one way or another. A number of them deal as well with the peculiar situation of the Australian writer, wandering in a byway that may soon become a main road.

I make no claims for the reflections that follow other than to say that they are one man's opinions on the nature of literature, and a record of his small, particular history as a novelist: an account of the way he thinks he's travelled. If some insights emerge concerning a larger history than my own, and if some of the enjoyment I've had in recording it has been communicated, I'm content.

Acknowledgements are due to the following publications, where the whole or parts of many of these pieces were first printed: *The Sydney Morning Herald*; *The Tasmanian Review*; *24 Hours*; *Westerly*; *Quadrant*; *The Launceston Examiner*; *The National Times*; *A Common Wealth of Words*; *The Age Monthly Review*; *Kunapipi*. Some passages from 'The Lost Hemisphere' appear in altered form in my novel *The Doubleman*.

C. J. K.
Sydney, August 1986

# Crossing the Gap

*Asia and the Australian Imagination*

I

In 1955, a year after our graduation from university, my friend Robert Brain and I set out for England. It was still the traditional pilgrimage for young Australians. We were returning to a home we had never seen: to the cultural Blessed Isles.

The yearly numbers who made the grand tour were steady but small, then. There was no question of going by air: economy jet travel was a thing of the future. That was the era of the ships – the gleaming, cloud-white passenger liners of P & O and Shaw Savill and Lloyd Triestino, and the sometimes less immaculate or downright dubious Greek and Italian vessels offering cheap passages to the young and poor. The names of those ships chime in the memories of whole generations of Australians born before 1945: the *Orcades*; the *Neptunia*; the *Fairsky*; the *Southern Cross*; the *Surriento*. Now that the age of the jet is totally established, and the only passenger ships still visiting the southern hemisphere are floating rest-homes for geriatric millionaires, aimlessly wandering the Pacific, it's left to one of my generation to give a farewell wave to those serious and thrilling workhorses that linked the two hemispheres – carrying us to the world, out of youth and into adulthood. They took a month and more to reach Europe; and this seemed only natural. After all, we were ploughing the curve of the globe from bottom to top, on the longest direct voyage in the world. Our ancestors on the sailing ships, convict and free, had taken many weeks longer coming the other way; so we thought ourselves fortunate.

Robert and I embarked on the *Surriento*, a Flotta Lauro boat bound for Genoa, via Jakarta, Singapore, Colombo and Suez. She was one of a fleet of tarted-up, creaking American Liberty ships left over from the War, bought by a Neapolitan tycoon and painted white, to signify their new incarnation as luxury liners. We were convinced; to us, the *Surriento* was glamorous as the *Orcades*, and boarding her, we felt ourselves to be adventurers. Saying so now seems quaint, when girl hitch-hikers from the middle-class suburbs of Melbourne and Sydney traverse the badlands of Turkey and Iraq; but in 1955, the phenomenon of Western youth touring the world on the cheap hadn't really begun.

The simplest way I can highlight this fact is to recall that when we reached Europe and began hitch-hiking, we had no trouble in being picked up because drivers found us a novelty. They also thought us adventurous; and as we passed farm gates, walking the highways of Italy and Germany, people would ask us in for a glass of wine. That was still the time when Greek peasants, finding foreigners passing their fields, would come out bringing gifts of food – the traditional hospitality to the wayfarer. They don't do it now; the hippies came through in the 1960s like a plague of locusts, living off that hospitality and abusing it until the tradition was ended forever.

In Britain, Australians still found amused tolerance and even good will, instead of weary hostility. That strange semi-fiction, that shadow of the British Empire called the Commonwealth, was something people actually took seriously: it was a rather nebulous, jokey family of nations, but it did give us some nice little advantages. The only formality we observed on entering Britain was to flip open our passports, which stated that we were Australian citizens and British subjects. We didn't have to have any money, which was just as well, since all I had left was the equivalent of one shilling and sixpence in Dutch coins; but that didn't matter, as work was easy to get, and I proceeded to clear tables in a Lyons Corner House, wearing a sort of dirty Cossack uniform. Nor was there any problem about length of stay, as our dual nationality was real. We were British, as I found out two years later, still in London: my call-up papers came, asking me to do two years' National Service on the Rhine. That was when I decided I'd better come home, if I was ever to do so.

I've recollected this youthful voyage not to discuss its European aspect, but to dwell on a detour that Robert and I made before reaching Europe: a detour which was then rather unusual. On an impulse, we had broken our journey at Colombo, disembarking from the *Surriento* with Mohindra Singh, a Sikh friend we had made on board, to travel the length of India from Ceylon to the Himalayas. This took us some months, during which we stayed for a time at Mohindra's home in New Delhi, eventually catching another Flotta Lauro boat on to Italy. And such a journey was hardly ever made in those days. Certainly it wasn't made by young men travelling rough.

The sixties were still to come; the hordes of truth-seekers hadn't yet taken the trail to Katmandu. Young Westerners simply didn't travel much in Asia; and that included young Australians. All that Australian voyagers saw of Asia was the ports, en route to their lost home in Britain; and what Robert and I were doing on the night we left the ship at Colombo was regarded as madness by the Australian and European fellow-passengers with whom we'd become friendly. Their faces, staring down from the rail, wore expressions of doubt and concern: I think they believed India would literally swallow us up. We'd catch diseases, they said.

We did, since we ate anything. And in all our travels through India, we scarcely saw other Europeans – except, from a distance, those on the diplomatic and business circuits in New Delhi. We saw no white faces at all on the trains, since we travelled second class, sleeping at night on the broad wooden luggage racks.

All my life I had dreamed of India; but India hadn't seemed within the bounds of the possible. I had scarcely imagined I might find myself there at twenty-two, and I travelled now in a sort of ecstasy; we both did. On the Grand Trunk Express, which took three days from Madras to Delhi, we were objects of great curiosity. This was only seven years after Independence; few British were touring here now, although the forms of British India were still almost intact, and we found we were seen as sahibs, Australian or not – and sahibs simply didn't travel second class. The Indians couldn't understand it; they were either amused or scandalised. On the second night, as more and more of them crowded into the compartment, things became rather hysterical; the sahibs lost their luggage-rack beds when they went out on the platform at one of the halts to buy cups of tea, and then had to sleep on the floor, as part of a tightly-packed arrangement of bodies. I spent one night with my head on a kindly old man's chest, his crate of fowls next to me.

We were travelling through an India where the British Raj had not yet gone away: we saw its ghost many times. It was an India I'm sure no longer exists, where two filthy and bedraggled young Australians were treated with a strange blend of giggling amusement and awe, and were still sahibs, enjoying a title and dignity they had no claim to and didn't want. We clowned, we made fun of ourselves, we insulted the British Empire; it was no use, the Indians smiled tolerantly, or else were genuinely shocked. The sahibs were joking; the sahibs merely chose to wear filthy shorts and sandals. We protested that we were almost broke; but our companions in the compartment were not fooled; they shook their head and knowingly smiled and smiled. We were sahibs – wealthy young men playing games. When we reached Dalhousie, one of those lovely Himalayan hill stations where the British had escaped from summer in the plains, we found a world undisturbed since 1947 and perhaps since 1907. No Europeans seemed to have come there since Independence; the place was preserved in amber. A procession followed us through the town, desperately trying to influence our choice as to which of the vast, empty hotels we would stay in. The one we chose gave us an apartment as big as a ballroom, and a magnificently turbaned and uniformed personal servant we called Rosie, who pressed our trousers and brought us tea in bed, like an Indian Jeeves. The whole thing cost seven and sixpence a night. The Indian Army, finding we were in town, gave us a superb dinner in the Officers' Mess. When we chose to go to the cinema, the manager would not allow the film to begin until we arrived, and then he would sit with us and explain it, in a loud drone. Old men salaamed us on the mountain trails. The sahibs had returned.

We had many conversations with Indians on our train journeys; and political freedom was recent enough for them to enjoy being good-humouredly rude to us about British rule, as though we somehow represented it – telling us how good it was the British had left. And there were some who were nostalgic, and said that the British should never have left. The Raj had been a two-way affair of love and hate; of this we were left in no doubt. In the end, with the thoughtless ease of the time and our youth, we half accepted the role they assigned to us: surrogate sahibs. What I did not consider then but am convinced of now, was that it was those Indians who were our brothers under the skin – not the British. We have turned out to share a similar destiny.

I am trying lately, like so many others in my country, to see where we belong in the new Asian–Pacific scene of this century's late decades. And since I'm a product of the British Empire, like all Australians of my generation, it may be that the way I've come since 1955 reflects in some small degree the way we've all come, we ex-colonials. We have drifted, it seems to me, across a suspension bridge made from three decades – a bridge that swings above that enormous gap between the end of an empire as ubiquitous as Rome's and our unknown future. It's a future where we figure as one of a conglomerate of Asian and Pacific powers, and where we find ourselves finally marooned in the southern hemisphere. Not much has happened yet, although President Sukarno threw a little scare into us. We have a breathing space, to decide who we are.

I don't have a neat answer to that question. If I did, I might be a good social analyst, but not, I think, a good novelist. A novelist is interested in such questions very much – but he comes at them sideways, since about thirty per cent of his activity is unconscious, and his material is the past. When he has re-worked the past, insights may emerge as to what it really contained; and these may cast shadows into the future.

2

Ten years after our Indian journey I published a novel, part of which was set there, entitled *Across the Sea Wall*. Few Australian writers had then set works of fiction in Asia, and it was not something I had anticipated doing. But the detour I had made into India had been, in a sense, a detour for life. Europe, to which I would return, was of poignant importance to me – but it was India I wrote about. It had exerted its fascination over me as it has done over so many who have been prepared to endure its climate and its comic and maddening trials; it had enmeshed my imagination. And so my fictitious characters played out their parts against the Javanese and Indian scenes that Robert Brain and I had explored on our first journey. But I was soon to find these scenes more than a backdrop.

In describing the voyage of the ship, north from Australia, I was charting the discovery of that world just over our fence, which we then seldom thought about and which lay between us and the northern hemisphere. It began with Indonesia, only a few days' sailing from Brisbane.

Jakarta was the first port of call on that voyage, and what was startling to my characters was that they had entered in those few days not just a new world geographically, but a whole different culture – having lived until now in a dream of ancestral Europe. But that dream was not purely a dream of Europe. Since it was a product of Empire, it included the Indian Empire; and the experience of India, unlike that of Indonesia, wasn't totally unexpected – it did have an echo; a familiar resonance. When I was twelve years old, convalescing from measles and not allowed to use my eyes, my father had read me the whole of Kipling's *Kim*, coming to my bedside each night. He had a gift for reading aloud, and no literary experience since has ever equalled it. I was in a spell, my senses altered by illness; India of the Raj hummed in my head, and odours of dust and marigolds filled the room. I would re-read the book again and again after that, following Kim and his Lama with all my heart along the Grand Trunk Road, in those wonderful passages that are surely among the best in English about India. It was the India of *Kim* I had looked for and found on the Grand Trunk Express; and I tried to reproduce that delight when I put my characters through a similar journey, in *Across the Sea Wall*.

Nothing in life really happens by chance, of course, and I had not been compelled to jump into India by accident. What had I looked for there? To follow Kim up the Grand Trunk Road, certainly; to seek an experience which in Kipling's day and in my childhood still lived under the shopworn title of 'romance'. But that was not all. In the fifties we had begun to take an interest in Indian religion: the beginning of that trend which in the sixties would burgeon into part of the mass youth culture based on California, London and New York. On the *Surriento*, Robert and I had fallen in with a group of young people of many nationalities: in addition to Europeans and Australians like ourselves, bound for Genoa, there were Asians returning home who had taken degrees at Australian universities, and who would get off, like Mohindra, at the ports along the way: Indonesians, Malays, Singapore Chinese and Indians. And everyone in our group was enthusiastically reading the *Bhagavad-Gita*: it was passed from hand to hand, a token which drew us together. It was to make a deep impression on me, and its delight has never waned. Working on *Across the Sea Wall*, I returned to the *Gita*; and as well, I began to read fairly extensively about Hinduism. I was particularly influenced, as other novelists have been before me, by Heinrich Zimmer and Sri Ramakrishna, and I began to find many meanings for my theme in the figures of Shiva and his consort of many names: the goddess who is called Durga and Devi and Kali and Parvati, and has in fact as many titles as she has facets, since she is the primordial power in the universe.

At that time, this figure had practically vanished from our consciousness, in the West. Once as omnipresent as Durga, with names just as various and mysterious, the ancient triple moon goddess of Europe was now a set of figments; she had been reduced to a collection of artefacts in museums, however eloquently Robert Graves might plead for her return. But a very different situation existed in India. There, I found, she was part of a living culture; and discovering her had the impact of the truly strange, and the force of unconscious recognition. She was woman as the incarnation of time and flux and destiny: the Indian counterpart of the White Lady we have banished from our days, but who still haunts our sleep. She was one of those whom the Australian Aborigines have so memorably described as the Eternal Ones of the Dream. As Kali – Ferry across the Ocean of Existence, womb and tomb, protectress and destroyer, eternal dancer – she was no mere folk creation, and no simple mother goddess, either. Her name itself meant Time, and she was the activating force in all things: śakti, stirring the dormant male principle from its quiet. This, it seemed, was the meaning of her eternal embrace with Shiva; and in the Gospel of Sri Ramakrishna, that seer and poet who was her most passionate disciple, I discovered the fullest revelation of her mysteries, and her identification with infinity: ākāśa, the void.

'Is Kali, my Divine Mother, of a black complexion? She appears black because she is viewed from a distance; but when intimately known she is no longer so . . . Bondage and liberation are both of her making . . . She is self-willed and must always have her way. She is full of bliss.' And: 'The Primordial Power is ever at play. She is creating, preserving and destroying in play . . .' And: 'My Divine Mother says: "It is I who make and unmake laws. I order all Karma, good and bad; come to me!"'

All the shifting subtleties of Hindu thought and vision proved to be embodied in this entity; and her cosmic dance, or 'play', as Ramakrishna called it, could bring pain and joy to humans with equal indifference, since the life force knows no morality, and is of double aspect. Hers was the infinite void in which India submerged itself, but from which the spirit of the West, with its need for classical limits and a frame, had always drawn back until now, sensing that demons and nightmares lurked there as well as bliss, and that pity there might prove to have no meaning.

Plainly unacceptable to Christianity, even in her persona as Artemis, this amoral and capricious divinity had nevertheless left a gap in Europe when she vanished underground. I'm cautious enough, remembering that she has often demanded blood, not to be tempted into calling for her resurrection, as Graves does, or suggesting that we worship her again, as some feminist thinkers like Nor Hall are lately doing. Dr Hall's book *The Moon and the Virgin* is one of the richest and most provocative of recent works on the Goddess, prophesying the triumphant return of the Mother and her mysteries and rituals into our psychic and social life; and when Dr Hall celebrates the latent power and ecstasy of the archetypal feminine in our unconscious, she is convincing, both at a poetic and psychological level. But she admits at one point, with honesty and insight, to extreme unease concerning a ritual of blood sacrifice offered to the Goddess by students at Santa Cruz, when Dr Hall was teaching there in the early seventies. At the time, she says, Californian interest in witchcraft and demon cults was 'at a frightening crest'; infants were said to have been sacrificed and eaten in Santa Cruz County in that year, and she contrasts the beauty of the Californian landscape with 'the paradoxical omnipresence of evil'. Her group planted a fig tree, buried a fish, crawled through an animal skin, invoked certain goddesses, and chanted hymns in their praise. 'These things I knew about,' says Dr Hall; but what disconcerted her was the spilling of a vial of human blood obtained from a research laboratory. 'By taking the sacrifice literally,' she says, 'we could have opened a door . . . to the wolf prowling there.'

Later, Dr Hall was reassured by her professor, who reminded her of the progression from bloody to bloodless sacrifice; from the literal to the spiritual body. This of course resembles the Christian exegesis in regard to communion, and the sacrifice of the Mass – but with the vital difference (for those who believe) that Christ was the actual sacrificial victim who ended forever both blood sacrifice itself and the compulsion to appease a fearsome or capricious Divinity – replacing this with a mystery based on love. And the Goddess herself, transformed as Mary, is the Mother of Mercy and intercessor for the human race: a Mother without caprice. But having said all this, it has to be admitted that when the Goddess of dual nature departed, she took away a symbolism which left the Western poetic imagination somewhat deprived, since she did so much to embody the paradox at the heart of life. And the more I learned of her, the more of a storehouse I found, for the purposes of my theme.

European writers had long found such a storehouse in the Greek and Roman myths; but for me, writing of a limited and unformed young Australian's journey into India, and of his obsession with a woman too alien, too flamboyant, too much of a troubled spirit for him to cope with, the mythology surrounding Hinduism's great goddess became more rewarding than anything in the Greco-Roman pantheon. In Tantrism, I discovered India's equivalent of the Dionysian mysteries and frenzies, and Kali would haunt both this novel and my next, since she seemed to me to symbolise so much about our current spiritual condition. Wasn't it Kali's void that the flower children were now taking passage to India in search of, with a little help from the Great God Pot?

Like many another writer, I was concerned with dualities. Perhaps an Australian writer must be a little more concerned with them than others are, since he is bound to find duality deep within his spirit. A European, he is forever severed from Europe, and unlike an American, is even severed from his ancestral hemisphere. As well, our age is an age of divisions, cultural, spiritual and psychological; they are within us all, so that even sexual postures are blurring and inverting. In Hinduism, I had found for the purposes of metaphor and symbol an entire system based on such dualities, personified by that figure who endlessly dances. And I concluded that Australia and India, in at least one way, might be akin in spirit. Australians might well become the Hindus of the south.

This notion was reinforced when I read Nirad Chaudhuri, the Bengali writer who has been a gadfly to his countrymen.

Chaudhuri wrote an autobiography when young (*Auto-biography of an Unknown Indian*) which ended in despair – 'a strange state of mind,' he says, 'for a young man of twenty-two'. Later in life, he diagnosed his own problem: in common with his fellow Hindus he was at odds with his own country, with the landscape into which he had been born. And this, he says, is because Hindus are Europeans in exile: Europeans whose ancestors wandered into the Indian plains from the cool grasslands of Hungary and the banks of the Danube, and who have never quite come to terms with the Dravidian spirit they have had to absorb – that spirit which Durga embodies. Hence the strange tensions in the Hindu soul. They were plainsmen, and so they settled the Indian plain; but they never adapted inwardly to the pitiless sun of the Deccan. They longed unconsciously for scenes forever lost.

And Chaudhuri goes on to make a startling call to his fellow Indians to recognise their true identity, saying that they will know no peace until they do. Having been opposed to British colonialism, he is opposed as well to 'brown colonialism' – dependence on foreign training and finance. With Quixotic passion, he calls for Indians to recover their own European spirit, to defer to no one, to dominate their environment themselves. The British, he says, were always seen wrongly as Europeans governing Orientals; instead, they were simply a new wave of European colonists, governing the earlier arrivals. And thus at a blow he explodes the notion of pathos in regard to Indians who are Europeanised: they are not trying to be 'Anglicised', he says: they are truly European in their souls, and colonised India 'as their collateral descendants did North America or Australia'.

Chaudhuri is a poet, seeking in himself the mysteries of his ancestral origins, and the myths and gods of his race. In his remarkable book, *The Continent of Circe*, I found strange correspondences to my own imaginative position in writing of India, and of the wandering Australian spirit. Where I, as a transplanted European Australian, had found metaphorical significance in the Indian goddess Durga, Chaudhuri, the transplated Indo-European, had found it in the Greek goddess Circe, who lured men with sweet music, but turned them into beasts. This, he says, is the danger India presents to all who come into the Deccan. It happened to the British, he claims, and quotes evidence of spiritual decline during their rule, such as a taste for pornography. The Hindu equivalent of this, he says, is such sex manuals as the Kamasutra, with which the West has been so impressed. These are symptoms of Hindu impotence and exhaustion, physical and spiritual. These are the wiles of Circe.

Naturally, not all of these themes of Chaudhuri's have met with a sympathetic response, at home or abroad. But those who have endured the Indian summer know that although India can be loved, it can also be appalling, and physically destructive. And those who have had any closeness with Indians can scarcely doubt the essentially European spirit that is within them. They are a river people; a cattle people. Nowhere does Chaudhuri express this more beautifully, at the deep level of the heart, than in the following passage, where he illustrates his central theme that the Hindu has a natural reverence for bucolic life. In this, Chaudhuri says, 'he shows himself to be a member of the great human family which spoke the Indo-European languages.' The hero–god Krishna typifies this, he says: an Aryan warrior who is also a cowherd. And he goes on to picture a farm in Bengal:

In the cult of cattle the deepest reverence and the most poetic quality were to be found in the daily routine, and that routine of care was at its best in relatively humble homes . . . The most charactcristic part of the ritual was the placing of the lamp in the cowshed at evening. At nightfall no room in a Hindu home could be without its lamp, for Sri, Grace of the world, shunned dark places . . .

The girl goes in, puts the lamp on a pillar of mud near the pen of the calves . . . There she stands still in reverie . . . The cows on their part stare at her, with their large liquid eyes . . . Animals do not feel grief. Yet tears of all things appear to gather in those eyes. At last a very faint voice comes borne on the darkness . . . 'Daughter! Come back to me from your dread Hades. Come back to Europe of the living. Come where you like – to snow-covered Russia, pine-covered Germany, or corn-covered Sicily. Only come back, Persephone, Persephone!'

Hot tears wet the cheeks of the Bengali woman. She could not have heard the call, or if she heard anything at all she could only have felt it as a deaf mute feels music by passing his hands over the baffle-cloth of his wireless set. Yet her heart is intolerably oppressed. She wipes away tears, and goes out of the hovel.

I am suggesting that many Australians inhabit the same spiritual region as that Bengali woman. Our consciousness of it may well increase, rather than decrease, as time goes on, since our course as a separate culture has only just begun, and a people needs a sense of origins and continuity as it needs dream and myth. No one needs it more than a country's artists. Without myth, the spirit starves, and in post-colonial Australia, we are going to have to build a new myth out of old ones. And I would suggest that these old ones will not belong simply to the European zone, but to the Indo-European zone, of which India and Indonesia are both inheritors, as we are. Other great cultures, such as China's, we may admire, we may gain from, but we will not find such family closeness with; the sense of common roots. Culture is a story, and we belong to the Indo-European story; we too are cattle people, as Les Murray has recognised in his poem 'Sanskrit':

> Around the sleeping house, dark cattle rubbing
> off on stiff corner joists their innocent felt
> and the house is nudged by a most ancient flow.
> I will wake up in a world that hooves have led to.
>
> To be of Europe also is a horn dance,
> cattle knowledge . . .

We tend lately to think in Australia of 'turning to Asia' – as though this were a new adaptation. But there is a sense in which we have always been conscious of Asia, since we began as part of that Empire whose linchpin was India. India was always there for our imaginations to roam in; and for this we largely have Kipling to thank. *Kim* alone, that gem among novels, can still tell us more about the Indian soul than any other English work except *A Passage to India*. That is not just my opinion of Kipling, but Nirad Chaudhuri's – and few Hindus are more critical of the British colonial mind than he is. It's interesting that Chaudhuri rejects the fashionable opinion that E. M. Forster truly respects and mirrors India while Kipling is a crass imperialist. Chaudhuri, in fact, deplores Forster's fundamental outlook as being condescending to Indians, whom, he says, Forster caricatures – a view, Chaudhuri says, that pleases only 'Indian toadies'. I was taken aback at this Hindu view of a writer I revere; but perhaps we ought to listen. And in contrast, this is what Chaudhuri has to say about Kipling – gently reminding us, at the same time, that his is the view of a 'Bengali Babu':

> I would set down, as a matter of moral obligation, that I consider Kipling to be the only English writer who will have a permanent place in English literature with books on Indian themes, and who will also be read by everyone who not only wants to know about *British* India, but also *timeless* India.

And in his discussion of the Indo-European tradition and the significance of Krishna, he says this:

> To those Western readers who wish to have the feel of this bucolic Krishna and yet cannot read the Krishna cycle in Sanskrit or Bengali I would recommend the few lines that Kipling has on him in his story 'The Bridge Builders'. I have not been able to understand how an Englishman . . . was able to get so near the essence of Vaishnava poetry.

Despite his imperial certainties – that hard shell he adopted to belong to the club – it becomes plainer with every biography and study of Kipling now appearing that his was a deeply troubled spirit, belonging nowhere in the end, because his inner life was truly Indian, not English. The account of his childhood in *Something of Myself* vividly shows why. The vital first six years of Kipling's life were spent in the care of an ayah in his parents' Bombay home, together with his sister; the nursery stories the ayah told them were Indian, and English was not even Kipling's first language:

> In the afternoon heats before we took our sleep, she or Meeta would tell us stories and Indian nursery songs all unforgotten, and we were sent into the dining room after we had dressed, with the caution 'Speak English now to Papa and Mamma.' So one spoke 'English', haltingly translated out of the vernacular idiom that one thought and dreamed in.

The treatment of the characters in *Kim* is equally revealing. Although there is a dutiful respect shown towards such English authority-figures as Colonel Creighton, they have a remote, somewhat two-dimensional quality, while the Orientals are realised with a warmth and richness that makes them unforgettable, and with an essential respect that springs from Kipling's deep involvement with their culture, Buddhist, Muslim and Hindu: that culture and legendry which had enmeshed his childhood. The Tibetan Lama; Mahbub Ali the horse dealer; Hurree Babu the Bengali secret agent – all are lovingly comprehended in a way that the colder English characters are not. And Kipling's contempt for blundering European ignorance of a whole different world and structure of beliefs in India is constantly conveyed through Kim's excursions between the two worlds of his origins, as well as in such scenes as the one where the Russian agent attempts to buy the Lama's drawing of the Wheel of Life. The Russian sees 'no more than an unclean old man haggling over a dirty piece of paper', which he tries to seize – little realising that he is insulting a Buddhist intellectual and gifted artist who is also, in his own country, a wealthy abbot. *Kim* is full of such things, and

the boy who is never sure whether he is English or Indian is
plainly Kipling himself.

Divisions again! If there is an equivalent in literature to the
products of the colonial Australian imagination, it is the work
of Kipling. Anglo-Indians and Anglo-Australians both had a
foot in two camps: in the one overseas that they were supposed
to love (truly their soul's country), and in the other that had
taken possession of them in childhood. Who can doubt which
had taken firmest hold of Kipling, listening to the Lama speak
to Kim when the River of the Arrow is found?

'Yea, my soul went free, and wheeling like an eagle, saw indeed that there was no Teshoo Lama nor any other soul. As
a drop draws to water, so my soul drew near to the Great Soul
which is beyond all things. At that point . . . I saw all Hind,
from Ceylon in the sea to the Hills . . . I saw every camp and
village . . . where we have ever rested. I saw them at one time
and in one place; for they were within the Soul . . . By this
I knew that I was free . . . As the egg from the fish, as the fish
from the water, as the water from the cloud, as the cloud
from the thick air; so put forth, so leaped out, so drew away,
so fumed up the soul of Teshoo Lama from the Great Soul.
Then a voice cried: "The River! Take heed to the River!"
. . . and I saw plainly the River of the Arrow at my feet.'

3

My next novel, *The Year of Living Dangerously*, was also set in
Asia, but closer to home: in Indonesia. I had not originally
intended to set it in Indonesia at all, but in Melbourne, the
book's main concern being to portray a man of double nature: a
man between cultures and beliefs, who sought answers to his

spiritual tensions by his faith in a famous leader. Worship of leader-figures, and what becomes of those who worship them, seemed to me a theme of some current significance; and I was interested in the fact that the worshippers are lately given to assassinating their idols. The dwarf cameraman, Billy Kwan, was the character in the book who was placed in this role, and from whom everything else sprang. Casting about for a leader with whom Billy could identify, I finally hit on President Sukarno of Indonesia, and everything fell into place.

A novelist must work with the material life gives him, and life had given me Sukarno. Years before, in 1968, while working as a radio producer in the Australian Broadcasting Commission, I had been seconded to UNESCO to carry out a mission in Indonesia, advising on the introduction of educational broadcasting to that country. Less than three years prior to that, on the night of 30 September 1965, the dramatic coup attempt had taken place that led to Sukarno's fall; and its after-effects still lingered in bankrupt Jakarta, which I found to be a city of rumours. Sukarno was still under house arrest up at Bogor, in what had been his dream palace; and one heard that he shuffled about in singlets and crumpled trousers, a broken man, the pride and the uniforms gone. Suspicion was in the air everywhere; the remnants of the Communists were still being rounded up in the countryside, and some of the Indonesians I worked with would whisper that this one or that one was ex-PKI.* In the Ramayana Bar of the Hotel Indonesia – at that time the only air-conditioned hotel in town, and a meeting place for foreign businessmen, adventurers and journalists – rumours were distilled and examined. Little had changed since the year of the coup.

* *Partai Kommunis Indonesia:* the Indonesian Communist Party.

That year fascinated me. Few nations see their destiny change overnight; yet this was what had happened to Indonesia, in those extraordinary twenty-four hours between the night of 30 September and the evening of 1 October 1965. I had often discussed the mysteries of coup night with my brother Philip, who had been the last Western correspondent still reporting from Jakarta when the attempt took place, and who had been placed under arrest in the presidential palace by the rebel troops. Some facts are clear, but the actual inception of the coup is still an enigma within an enigma, which may never be solved.

In a series of pre-dawn raids in the suburbs of Jakarta, the September Thirtieth Movement – a group of army officers backed by the PKI – kidnapped and murdered six of Indonesia's top army generals. The presidential palace and the radio station were seized, and a revolutionary headquarters was set up out at Halim Air Force Base, where the coup leaders – including D. N. Aidit, head of the PKI – were gathered. They were joined in the morning by Sukarno himself; and this was a fatal move for the president, since he was seen to have given the coup his blessing. When evening came, the coup was in ruins, its leaders had fled and the remorseless process that followed saw the extinction of the PKI, the violent death of Aidit, and the slow disgrace and political emasculation of Sukarno – that magnetic, paradoxical figure who had virtually created modern Indonesia, and who is surely, whatever his failings, one of the great leaders of the twentieth century.

Why had he joined the plotters at Halim, on that morning of 1 October? This remains the central mystery of the coup, and the Bung has taken the answer to his grave – on which they have finally carved the simple inscription he wanted:

'Here lies Bung Karno, mouthpiece of the Indonesian
People.'

In the days of struggle, and in the early years of independence, he had truly been that and more. He had led his people
to freedom from Dutch colonial rule; he had been worshipped,
from Java to the most remote islands of the archipelago, as few
leaders have ever been worshipped. His charisma, his humour,
his jaunty charm, his intoxicating oratory and his poetic flair all
made him irresistible. But in his decline, Bung Karno had
become yet another of these demagogues with which our
century is all too familiar: a sort of Indonesian Mussolini,
feeding his people on fantasies of violence and conquest
instead of rice; dragging the country to bankruptcy and ruin.
The process had about it all the elements of Greek tragedy.

But it wasn't my purpose to tell Sukarno's story; nor to write
a documentary novel about the year he had prophetically
entitled the Year of Living Dangerously. What I set out to do
was to place my fictitious characters and their fictitious story
within the frame of that piece of recent history and that year;
and I wanted Sukarno to cast his shadow over their lives, rather
in the way that Napoleon was made to do by such nineteenth-
century novelists as Tolstoy and Stendhal. The more I studied
him, the more I realised that he was an ideal figure with whom
Billy Kwan could identify, since Sukarno was very much a man
of dualities: both Hindu and Muslim by birth; poet and
demagogue; a member of the aristocratic *priyayi* class, and yet a
man of the people – a socialist. Billy saw Sukarno as his alter
ego. He also saw Guy Hamilton in this way: the tall, handsome and uncomplicated correspondent for whom he worked.
And in these two, I found myself devising a sort of double
hero, since Kwan, the tormented Australian-Chinese, and

Hamilton, the cool English-Australian, were two aspects of the one: mystic and simple soul, thinker and man of action; both of them products of a dying colonial world.

We may think of Indonesia as a deeply traditional society, which in many ways it is; but in others it resembles Australia, being a Pacific country which is an ex-colony – not just of Holland, but culturally of India and Arabia. Like Australia, it's in certain ways a country of second-hand. The Asian cultures have been grafted on: Islam; Hinduism; the court life of Java; and Sukarno was aware of all this. Despite being very Javanese in his nature and background, he was imbued with the dynamic tradition of Europe through his voracious youthful reading; and the concept he called Marhaenism was an original and impressive attempt to formulate, in the European manner, a peculiarly Javanese social philosophy: an answer to Marxism. Marhaen was a small peasant landowner whom Sukarno met in his youth – a man working less than a third of a hectare of land, owning nothing else but his tools. He was a pauper and yet a landowner; and Sukarno maintained that Marhaen was truly representative of the struggling Indonesian people. The dispossessed industrial proletariat on whom Marxism was based, who had only their labour to sell, belonged to the cities of nineteenth-century Europe; they had little relevance to the rural poor of South-East Asia. It was Marhaen, Sukarno said, whom he must lead to freedom.

There is an interesting story told of Sukarno: that on a walk in the hill town of Lembang, near Bandung, he said: 'Where are the great works we have produced?' And he spoke of the sacred Hindu epic *Mahabharata*, and of Gothic cathedrals. 'The Indian, Chinese and Western cultures are three-dimensional,' he said. 'Ours is two-dimensional.'

He was probably in one of his low moods; in others, he would take pride in the artistic nature of his people, and in Indonesia's cultural monuments, such as the great pyramid temple of Borobudur. But the remark about two-dimensionalism intrigued me; for one thing, he probably had in mind the *wayang kulit*, the ancient shadow play: and there is a truth in his remark which is essentially poetic rather than social.

When I wrote my novel, I made a study of the *wayang*; and I found myself led back again to the Hindu world: to the gods of Hinduism, and the heroes of its epics; in short, to the Indo-European storehouse. The classical *wayang* plays are based on the great cycles from the *Ramayana* and the *Mahabharata*, and here were familiar figures: figures from my childhood reading, strangely transformed into darting shadows. Here were the Pandava brothers, from my book of Indian legends; and Devi-Durga-Kali reappeared as Dewi Sri, the Goddess of Rice. Sukarno himself was seen as Vishnu's incarnation, riding his helicopter-car.

And so that trail that had been found in India wound back through Java to the shores of Australia, where it is waiting for all of us, if we take an interest in the broader Indo-European heritage that is ours. Like the Indonesians, we are now essentially a Pacific people who inherit a culture from the northern hemisphere; we have more in common than we imagine. And if, like me, a writer is myth-obsessed, whole new metaphors and symbolic patterns are made possible. When Joyce gave *Ulysses* a sub-structure based on Homer's *Odyssey*, he introduced a device with rich possibilities for the novel; taking this as my model, I found I was able to utilise a classical Indonesian *wayang* play, *The Reincarnation of Rama*, all the episodes of which correspond to the progressions in my book: the opening court scenes; the hero's pilgrimage to the hills in search of enlightenment; the consequent turmoil in nature, and the final conflict of the *wayang* of the left and the *wayang* of the right, followed by the planting of the Tree of Life. And Hamilton and Kwan came to have distinct correspondences with Prince Arjuna and his faithful dwarf Semar, from the Pandava cycle.

With Indonesia in particular, we in Australia have a future to invent together. There will always be profound differences, cultural and religious – but these may lessen, as we absorb one another's systems of thought and belief. And there is a yearning, I think, among some Indonesians, that we should pursue the story of our related cultures together – those cultures which began to the north of us both. We should not ignore that yearning. The future we face in the Pacific may be dangerous, but I suspect it will be anything but dull.

# 'Maybe It's Because
I'm a Londoner'

*The cold became intense. In the main street, at the corner of the
court, some labourers were repairing the gas pipes, and had lighted
a great fire in a brazier, round which a party of ragged men and
boys were gathered: warming their hands and winking their eyes
before the blaze in rapture. The water-plug being left in solitude,
its overflowings sullenly congealed, and turned to misanthropic ice.
The brightness of the shops, where holly sprigs and berries crackled
in the lamp heat of the windows, made pale faces ruddy as they
passed. Poulterers' and grocers' trades became a splendid joke . . .*
Charles Dickens, A Christmas Carol

*'So much for the Lascar manager. Now for the sinister cripple who
lives upon the second floor of the opium den, and who was certainly
the last human being whose eyes rested upon Neville St Clair.'*
Sir Arthur Conan Doyle, Adventures of Sherlock Holmes

*I saw the Chinaman with the branded forehead, and remembering
what Fomalhaut had told me, I decided that this man could be no
other than the chief of the Gang.*
Frank H. Shaw, 'The Brand of Mystery' (*Chums*, 1920)

I

London, in my earliest days, came to me always as a set of
images by night.

It was a night more thrillingly cold and vast than any in
Tasmania, congested with huge, grimy buildings of ineffable
importance, and with grimly hurrying people whose concerns

were those of a metropolitan Valhalla. It was half fearsome, its alleys the haunt of blackjack-wielding thugs and of various grotesques: hunchbacks, criminal cripples and deformed beggars. The sirens of ships sounded alarmingly from the Pool of London. And yet it had pockets of warmth and enviable snugness, glowing through the fog: gas lamps flaring beside old doorways of worm-eaten wood; candles in attic windows above inn yards, staining the thick northern air with yellow. In rooms where great fires blazed in open fireplaces that were larger and more efficient than ours, men in dinner suits gave low-voiced directions for the running of the world. Mr Pickwick had warmed his coat-tails before such fires; Christopher Robin was made cosy by them, safe in his nursery; and boys much more worldly-wise than my brother and I toasted sausages and muffins over the coals. Sherlock Holmes and Dr Watson, hurrying through pea-soupers to their rooms in Baker Street, could always be confident that a blazing fire awaited them.

This unique British snugness in things – an aspect of the imperial ability to tame a naughty world – was readily and vicariously shared in the freezing Hobart winters of my childhood. And other, more disturbing flames flickered in our imaginations in those days: the bonfires lit by the Blitz. The fires of London, snug or apocalyptic, glowed at the distant centre of our universe, since London was the City: the capital of the world. There was no other city that mattered; Melbourne and Sydney were mere towns, and New York was rumoured to be a brash monstrosity. London was both the city of cities, and the all-wise, half-forbidding Friend.

All this began earlier than I can remember. My Grandfather Hurburgh, in those infant years before I could read, used to take the old *Strand Magazine*, where Sherlock Holmes had still been making his appearance not so many years before. On its cover was a picture of the famous street, and this is my most ancient and central memory of London. I somehow saw my Tasmanian grandfather – who had never been farther than Sydney, but whose own grandfather had come from Greenwich – as a Londoner; once, I believed, he had walked the Strand itself, in his gleaming black shoes, as all heroes of the city must do. Its deep and splendid channel, crowded with shining cars and godlike city people, was the thoroughfare of destiny we all must some day tread, to pass beneath its porticoes and pinnacles of filigreed stone. And very early too – so early that it has become like a memory of my own past – I followed Ebenezer Scrooge to that 'gloomy suite of rooms, in a lowering pile of buildings up a yard' where Marley's ghost awaited him.

Like many another child of the Empire in the thirties, I had been named after Christopher Robin; *When We Were Very Young* had been read to me when I was three. My brother and I had Dickens read to us when we were seven and nine years old, and Oliver Twist and Pip and Little Nell and Mr Bumble were famous figures we might some day meet: our parents and relatives spoke of them as though they were real, and I can still see my mother pursing her lips over Uriah Heep. 'Give us a child until the age of seven.' It wasn't the Jesuits who had us until that age, it was Christopher Robin, Buckingham Palace, Little Pig Robinson, Mr Toad, Sherlock Holmes, and a school called Clemes College. Our teachers made us keep scrapbooks on the doings of 'the little princesses', Elizabeth and Margaret Rose. What chance did we have?

Clemes College was a decaying private school where our father and his brother had gone, housed in a musing nineteenth-century building with french windows leading from the kindergarten room onto an antique sandstone terrace, surrounded by English gardens in which stone urns gathered English moss. It was run by old, vague, white-moustached Mr Clemes, who was English, and by a staff of English maiden ladies who smiled a lot but who displayed sadistic tendencies, setting about us with rulers, and watching with gleaming eyes as big boys tortured smaller ones in the playground. These ladies read us *Alice in Wonderland* and *The Jungle Book*, and pointing to a globe of the world in the corner of the classroom, showed us how red was the dominant colour on the map, a pattern ending at the bottom with the little red shield of Tasmania. We were left in no doubt of what we were and where we were; being Australians was secondary, and at the top of the map, in the south of that dragon-shaped island we had never seen, the great web of London waited for us to come to it.

My earliest expeditions through London were made in the pages of *Chums*: an ancient British boys' paper which finally expired in the early years of my childhood, before the Second World War. I had inherited *Chums Annual* for 1920 from my cheerful Uncle Gordon, who had owned it when he was my age, and who would be off next year to New Guinea in the AIF, to fight the Japanese. 'Some of those stories'll give you the dingbats,' he warned me, and I thrilled in anticipation of being terrified. I was not to be disappointed: a pirate story called 'The Night Rovers' was to petrify me as no literary work has done since:

It sounded quite loud, for one of the small panes was broken, and I counted thirteen taps. Then they ceased, and a most horrible chuckle ended with a low whistle.

'Thirteen!' breathed a voice that made me shiver. 'That was your number, Cutlas, when we drew lots. And mine was seven. Thirty years agone on the Spanish Main . . .'

Boys must have read more in the 1920s, I decided, as I gloated over the sheer size and weight of this big red book – understanding for the first time the full, pregnant meaning of the word 'volume'. It was actually a bound collection of weekly papers, giving off a delicate scent of age: the antiquity that was twenty-one years ago. Each yellowing newsprint page contained three columns of tiny type, with old-fashioned headings; black and white illustrations occurred, but they did little to interrupt the marvellous, almost limitless fields of print. This book, I saw immediately, would take years to exhaust, and I was right; when my uncle came back safe from the war, whistling around the house in his jungle greens, there were still stories in *Chums* I hadn't read.

At nine and ten years old, one of life's chief ecstasies was to sit up in bed on a winter's night with *Chums* propped on my knees, a cup of cocoa in my hand, the westerly wind rushing in the big pine tree next door, rain drumming on the iron roof of the sunroom my brother and I shared as a bedroom. Of course, as we now know, such papers were tainted with the quaint and objectionable prejudices and myths of their era. Hearty xenophobia, as well as a mystical devotion to the British Empire, were confidently expected of their boy readers; but I knew little then about the ramifications of such things. My friends and I took it for granted that Chinese were sinister, and called 'Chinamen'; that the only good savages in 'the heart of Africa' were those who devotedly served clean-living young English Bwanas; that Dutchmen (the Boer War having left its mark) were treacherous. I tended to skip the self-improvement and athletic articles ('Boxing for Boys'), and to concentrate on the serials, many of them written by men with military titles (Captain Oswald Dallas; Major Charles Gilson). There were pirate stories, heart-of-Africa stories, Canadian backwoods stories; but dominating everything, and fascinating me most, were stories whose background was the city of London.

In the year that *Chums* came into my hands, London was enduring the Blitz, and we thought of the city now with a protective concern. As I sat up in bed reading 'The Night Rovers', bombs were hitting Westminster Abbey, the Houses of Parliament, and the Wren churches we sang about in 'Oranges and Lemons' in the Clemes College playground. Images of all this came to us through photographs and the cinema, the dome of St Paul's glowing inviolate at the centre of destruction, ringed by defiant searchlights and anti-aircraft guns. We never doubted in Tasmania that London would win; never doubted that the Spitfires would triumph over the Messerschmitts and the Junkers 88s. We listened with a lump in our throats to the unperturbed, paternal voice of the BBC announcer speaking from the heart of fire and terror, on the late-night broadcast carried by the ABC. 'This is London calling.' It was a voice made to waver only by the fluctuations of short wave, and by the global distance that separated us from our capital. The droning of the German bombers filled our heads as though they were only miles off; by 1942 our own windows were covered with blackout blinds, and air-raid practice at night made the war come even closer. Sirens brayed and searchlights swept across the sunroom windows as we waited for an invasion by imperial Japan. Our fate now depended on America, and on a straggling line of Australians in slouch hats (Uncle Gordon among them) on the Kokoda Trail; but it also depended on the war in Europe. Tasmanians flew in the Lancasters and Halifaxes that bombed the Ruhr.

Those who have not been subjects of a global empire, who have not been made aware from infancy of what were then called 'ties of blood', will never understand these far-off things. No English man or woman will ever be able to experience what a colonial Australian or New Zealander of British or part-British descent felt about England. We were subjects of no mortal country; hidden in our unconscious was a kingdom of Faery: a Britain that could never exist outside the pages of Hardy, Kenneth Grahame, Dickens and Beatrix Potter; and yet it was a country we confidently set out to discover. We sailed, as soon as we reached our twenties, for isles of the Hesperides we never doubted were real. What no native of the 'mother country' could ever understand – what no one but overseas children of the Empire could ever experience, in fact – was the unique emotion summoned up by the first sight of a country known at one remove from birth, and waited for as an adolescent waits for love. We really did stare at the white cliffs of Dover with beating hearts; we really did survey London (familiar yet unfamiliar, in a dreamlike, paradoxical mix), with a surge of intoxication. This quickly wore off, as the cold realities of bedsitters and jobs descended on us; but nothing could rob us of those first hours and weeks.

These are archaic emotions, now. No doubt citizens of the imperial Roman possessions once experienced them, on coming into Rome for the first time. Possibly they will never be felt again. But those who dismiss them as a sentimental absurdity have no conception of their intensity, and fail to understand the central convictions and fantasies that history can brew up, shaking whole generations with their poignancy; making them willing to die for such fancies. Afterwards, as a joke, they are made to be merely quaint.

2

For me, the London of fancy became the London of fact at the age of twenty-two; and by pure chance, my entry was made via the Strand. Robert Brain and I, penniless after hitch-hiking about Europe, had landed in England at Harwich, having come across by ferry from the Hook of Holland. We caught the train to London, and entered the tube system, to emerge into the city's open air at Charing Cross Station.

Here was the Strand then, on a fine summer's morning, carrying its human streams towards the Aldwych, St Clement Danes and the Inns of Court and Chancery where Dickens's Lord High Chancellor had sat at the heart of the fog, and no doubt sat still. Here were men actually wearing black morning-coats, pin-striped trousers and bowler hats, wielding furled umbrellas, whom we examined with joy, until one of them glared at us. Here was a real copy of *The Times*, bought from an actual, cloth-capped Cockney at the entrance of the station, who called Robert 'Guv'nor'. A man passed us now clad in a suit of green silk, wearing a green top hat and talking to himself. He was an unusual sight to young Tasmanians in 1955, but no one else in the crowd even glanced at him: here was the famous British tolerance of eccentricity. We entered Forte's café across the road, where we drank without complaint a grey liquid called coffee which was certainly not coffee; then, in a daze of delight, we wandered on under the promised porticoes and pinnacles of filigreed stone. There was Villiers Street, running down to the Embankment, where we might well have to sleep out, we knew, if we didn't find jobs immediately. And here, reassuringly, was Tasmania House, where we went in to the desk and found our mail awaiting us. This was our club, and London was already our home.

But if it was home, it was a stern and tight-fisted one. For the first time, we understood our good fortune simply in being born Australian. Post-war Australia was carefree and prosperous; post-war Britain was grim and poor; these facts were soon borne in on us, as we contemplated weekly wages which at home would barely have satisfied us as pocket money, and nearly half of which would be needed to rent a single bedsitting room. London was still marked by the Blitz: war-damaged buildings were being repaired, and flowers grew on the gaping bomb-sites. An air of austerity persisted, and people had the manner of cheerfulness in adversity: that style we had become familiar with in wartime British films. Faced with these realities, we soon separated. Robert landed a job in one of the counties, teaching in a summer school; and I found myself alone in London.

At that time, the new Welfare State didn't pay unemployment benefits which made survival possible; nor did one think of applying for them. I must quickly find work or starve; I had five pounds borrowed from Robert to stave off that eventuality, and my search began. Tramping the streets, gazing up at lighted windows in Charing Cross Road, Piccadilly and the Bayswater Road, peering through the doorways of buildings whose intimidating neo-Greek façades forbade entry to any shabby young colonial, I began to understand what the American writer Thomas Wolfe had discovered here before me: that there were two races in England, the Big People and the Little People.

These were the days before large-scale immigration from India and the West Indies, and the island's two indigenous races were very clearly recognisable; I was seeing, although I didn't know it, the last of the frozen old England which the post-imperial era was dissolving. The Big People, who ate in restaurants in Mayfair and Soho where the prices terrified me, were conveyed past in Jaguars and Rovers and Rolls Royces, and lived in another London than the one I was discovering. My London was the London of the tiny bedsitter in Bayswater or Earl's Court or Notting Hill Gate, with its gas-ring for cooking, gas-meter to pay coins into, aged washbasin and shared, freezing bathroom down the passage. 'Your bath will be on Tuesdays and Thursdays,' my first landlady informed me. 'Mr Drummond has his on Mondays and Wednesdays, and Miss Appleby has hers the other days.' My London was the London of the cheap caf, with sausages, eggs and chips for two and sixpence, and tea for fourpence. It was a London whose streets were the grey of old overcoats, its buildings of that liver-coloured brick whose hue seems the essence of despair; the districts of *Little Dorrit*:

> Wildernesses of corner houses, with barbarous old porti-
> coes and appurtenances, horrors that came into existence
> under some wrong-headed person in some wrong-headed
> time . . . Rickety dwellings . . . like the last results of the great
> mansions breeding in-and-in . . .

This London, into which I was descending like so many other young Australians, was the London of the Little People: Cockneys and working-class Londoners who received us with the friendliness of fellow-spirits. Cockneys in particular assumed that an Australian was a sort of lost tribal brother, and one felt that this was so. The Little People existed with few creature comforts, keeping their clothes neat and maintaining an unaccountable jauntiness. They didn't own the houses they lived in; they had no cars; they could afford no holidays, except for a few days at Brighton; their only pleasures were a few pints of bitter in the evenings and a seat in the cinema or the music hall once a week. And this life was soon to be mine.

The interview for my first job held a promise of glamour. It was conducted by a pretty young employment officer at Lyons Corner House, where I had applied to wash dishes. She spoke in the accents of the Big People. 'Hev you ever appeared before the public?'

No, I said cautiously, I hadn't.

'Do you maind appearing before the public?'

No, I didn't mind; and I was issued with the grey, vaguely Cossack jacket which was the required uniform of a Lyons waiter, and sent out on the floor to what was called a 'station'. This was a block of tables which it was my duty to keep cleared of dirty crockery, and where my other task was to pour tea and coffee for the customers. The kitchen, reached through swinging doors, was a tiled ante-chamber to Hell; here I fought through a line of other snarling waiters to keep my coffee and tea pots filled at the huge, hissing urns. But outside, on the red-carpeted floor, all was grandeur.

Lyons Corner House at the corner of Tottenham Court Road and Oxford Street, long vanished, was really just a big self-service restaurant. But it provided elegance; it was a place where the Little People could pretend to be Big People, helped by the fact that after they had queued for their meals, their tea and coffee were poured for them by waitresses, or by uniformed men such as myself. A big Hammond organ was played by a man in a dinner jacket in the afternoons, and the whole scene was patrolled by a species of floor-walker: men in frock coats and striped trousers who were our immediate superiors, and who kept us up to the mark. They too, I realised from their accents, were technically Little People, but they were physically large and martial-looking and had an air of haughty menace that was very intimidating, lining us up each morning for a military inspection.

'Koch, your uniform's filthy. Get a fresh one.'

'Sir.'

I earned five pounds a week, and my bedsitter in Notting Hill Gate cost three; it was not really enough to survive, but on Friday, which was payday, Lyons allowed us a free meal. I had worked out that by Thursday I could usually afford either to eat or to smoke; being addicted to cigarettes then, I chose to smoke. Lying in bed on a Thursday night, my stomach rumbling, dragging deeply on a Woodbine (the cheap fag of the Little People), I would think about the free meal in the kitchen next day, which included nauseating cream cakes. Like many of the Little People, I allowed myself a half pint of bitter in the pub in the evening, a picture show a week, and ten cigarettes a day; these pleasures being digested with miserly care. I should have been miserable, but I wasn't; a vast elation would seize me at unexpected moments. My love affair with the real London had begun.

I had begun to comprehend that this city of cities, despite its grim façades and its penny-pinching and its beggars, was strangely gentle. The gold light of October fell on sooty, golden stone, and on a hundred gently-frowning little church spires, and I began to understand too what every newcomer here learned: that it was really a set of villages, and that one of its great virtues was a fond, village cheerfulness. Cockney bus conductors impersonated comedians on the double-deckers that took me along Oxford Street in the mornings; motherly women in shops called me 'dear', and I saw that people smiled at each other far more than they did in any Australian city. One Sunday morning in that autumn, I was woken in my room in Ladbroke Square by the sound of a tune, floating through the window from the street below: 'Maybe it's because I'm a Londoner':

> 'I get that funny feeling inside of me
> Just walking up and down.
> Maybe it's because I'm a Londoner
> That I love London town . . .'

I knew who was playing it: a group of street musicians I'd often seen trudging along the kerb in the Bayswater Road: a one-armed, straw-haired trumpeter, an old accordionist with a black Homburg hat; a thin violinist in a long muffler. I had heard this ballad in an earlier life, it seemed to me, and I knew, in my Sunday bed, that in some way I already belonged to the London of my ancestors, and would do so forever.

I had now begun to make friends. My first friends were two show-business men down on their luck: Derek, a Canadian tap-dancer working with me in Lyons, and his friend Buddy, a New Zealand accordionist. They shared a shabby double room in Camden Town, home of Bob Cratchit, where Buddy would cook us elaborate Sunday roasts. Later I would make English friends, but for now, we three outcasts from the old Dominions wandered about London in our time off, sharing our loneliness. Derek and Buddy, I came to realise, had no friends other than me.

'They'll never let you into their homes,' Buddy told me, discussing the English. 'Never. Just realise that from the start.' A bald, stout old man of around sixty, always in a brown felt hat, he had a high, chanting voice and a dolefully dogmatic air, and was very bitter against the world. He was now working on a counter in an Oxford Street department store; it had been some years, I gathered, since he had played his accordion around the music halls, and I suspected that he would never be hired again. He put his troubles down to corrupt theatrical agents who refused to book him.

'Those bloody agents,' he would say. 'They take bribes. They work their favourites into the halls, and leave better performers to starve. If I could shoot them all, I would; every one of the greasy bastards. The barrel of my rifle would be running *hot*, and still I'd be blazing away.' His mouth worked, as he stared into vistas of carnage.

'Now Buddy,' Derek would say soothingly. 'You're just workin' yourself up.' He was a thin, pale, sweet-natured man in his thirties, with thin blond hair, who always referred to himself as 'a hoofer'. He too hadn't been hired for some time, and I wondered if he would ever hoof again.

Buddy and Derek introduced me to the music halls: one of the cheap pleasures that London then offered the Little People. For ninepence, we could go upstairs at Collins' Music Hall or the old Finsbury Park Empire and watch jugglers, comedians, dancers, and vocalists like Dicky Valentine. Buddy and Derek would whisper professional comments in the dark, staring down at the lemon-lit stage from which they were exiled.

'*His* voice is going. Straining it, you can tell.'

'Without a mike, *she'd* be nothing. No power at all.'

'Poor old bastard, his back's giving him trouble. See that?'

'Now *there's* a lovely hoofer.'

'Fifty, if he's a day. Bribed the agent, I'll bet.'

'Now Buddy, don't be bitter. You'll only give yourself a heart condition.'

'Agents. My barrel would be running *hot*.'

'Buddy, please. We're trying to hear the vocalist.'

I now found a job at a pound a week more, in the Hearts of Oak Insurance Company at Euston; and the last edges of the world of Dickens closed even more firmly about me.

At the Hearts of Oak, I found myself in a large room surrounded by glass offices, sitting at a long wooden table together with some eight or ten other men. Our job was addressing and sealing envelopes; we did nothing else. This was carried out with steel-nibbed pens, dipped into a set of common ink-wells. I eventually asked one of the supervisors why typewriters weren't used, and he reacted with distaste. 'The Hearts of Oak would never treat its customers like that. They expect the personal touch.' What went into these envelopes, I discovered, were reminders that premiums were due.

We were supervised by a group of men who appeared, like their counterparts in Lyons Corner House, to be floor-walkers. They wore the same black morning coats and striped trousers, they were large and intimidating, walked with their hands behind their backs, and spoke in the accents of the Big People. They patrolled past our table at regular intervals, bringing us to order.

'Mr Brown, that's enough talking. Resume your work.'

'Mr Koch, have you no more envelopes? Then why are you speaking to Mr Dempsey?'

What other functions these men had, and the true nature of their work, still remain a mystery to me. They disappeared for long periods, but were always hovering in the background, like suave crows.

On my first day, I made an error I was not to make again. Having collected a set of envelopes and a list of names to be copied from a man who sat at a desk on a sort of podium, I took them away, finished them in an hour, and brought them back to him.

'What's this?' he said.

'I've finished.'

He stared at me in weary disbelief. 'Try to understand, Koch. That was your morning's work.'

I understood. Going back to the table, I realised that I would have time here to loaf and invite my soul; even perhaps to tinker with a chapter of the first novel on which I was working at night. We were a happy band of men at that table, all quietly aware of the gift of leisure the Hearts of Oak was giving us – provided, like good children, we were not too noisy, and pretended to write when the supervisors came past. We did crosswords and the football pools; told each other the stories of our lives; discussed films we'd seen; told dirty jokes; debated politics and philosophy, and smoked our Woodbines – always bent over our envelopes, our pens describing writing motions. My chief friends were Bill Brown, an ex-tail-gunner who had flown many raids over Germany, and who now found civilian life boring, and Mr Dempsey, a little old Irish gentleman who had lost all his money.

Handsome, diminutive and gnomish, Mr Dempsey had a sweeping mane of white hair, a trim white moustache, brilliant blue eyes, and a patrician bearing that was probably quite unconscious. He dressed nearly always in a tweed suit of excellent quality which I suspected was the last of a stylish wardrobe. He was, he told me, nearly seventy, well past retiring age, but the Hearts of Oak had taken him on three years ago as a favour, when he lost the last of his assets. He preferred to work rather than draw the pension, on which he and his wife would have found it difficult to survive. Always perky, despite his descent in the world, he was full of extraordinary schemes for escaping the Hearts of Oak and making money. He formed a sort of grandfatherly fondness for me, and seemed to believe that he and I would carry out one of these schemes together. Perhaps it was just a game; but if it was, he never let on. His optimism was supernatural.

'I've had a wonderful notion, my dear,' he said one morning. 'We'll sell bicycles to the Americans. Bill here agrees it would work.'

This scheme, the details of which I've forgotten, occupied us for over a week, with detailed plans and figures on Hearts of Oak stationery. When he got particularly excited, Dempsey would spring to his feet and quote from the poem which he said had provided the firm's name, declaiming it at the top of his voice. 'Hearts of Oak, the Captain cried!'

A black-coated figure would loom up. 'Mr Dempsey, what is the trouble?'

'Sorry, sir – just loyally quoting the firm's motto.'

When Dempsey discovered me to be an aspiring writer, furtively at work on a novel on the backs of premium forms, he became even more enthusiastic. 'You must write down your impressions of England *now*, my dear, while they're fresh. Young people like yourself from the Dominions see us with new eyes. You ought to get it down before it fades. Get it down.'

His insistence had a personal note; and over the weeks and months, I came to feel that he looked to me to fulfil some lost dream of his own.

His story was at first unbelievable to me. He came from a wealthy Anglo-Irish family, and over a lifetime – perhaps through wild schemes – had run through his entire inheritance. But he had no regrets, he said; he'd enjoyed his adventures, and now and then he gave me glimpses of life on the Riviera in the thirties, where he had met his French wife. 'The casinos were my downfall,' he said quietly, dipping into the inkwell. 'I lost a lot there. Well, well, easy come easy go, my dear, and we must be grateful to the Hearts of Oak for giving us our sustenance.' He rose to his feet and raised his steel-nibbed pen on high. 'Hearts of oak, the Captain cried!'

'Mr Dempsey. These outbursts really must stop.'

'Aye, aye, sir. Just reciting the firm's motto. We are all grateful to the firm.'

He had written his autobiography, he told me, which had been published some years ago by Hutchinson. He had been friends with Alexander Korda, and had put some money into a film of Korda's, shot on the Black Sea. Secretly, I decided that these were the fantasies of a poor little old man who was merely a clerk; I even began to wonder if he had ever had any money. But one day he brought me a copy of the book he had written, published by Hutchinson, sure enough: and there, among others, was a photograph of a youthful Dempsey with Alexander Korda, on location on the Black Sea.

'Yes, it's all true,' Bill Brown said to me disgustedly. 'The mad little bastard ran through all his money. And now he's ended up here. Serve him right; if *I'd* had that money I'd have bloody well hung on to it.'

But Mr Dempsey's cheerfulness began now to seem to me heroic. He loved poetry, and when I asked him whether he was ever downcast about his fate, he quoted Housman to me:

'Be still, my soul, be still; the arms you bear are brittle,
Earth and high heaven are fixt of old and founded strong.
Think rather, – call to thought, if now you grieve a little,
The days when we had rest, O soul, for they were long.

'That's what I tell myself when unhappiness or discontent come upon me,' he said, 'and you should learn to do the same. Tell your soul to be still, and it will be. All bad things pass, my dear, just like all good things. They pass.'

Eventually Mr Dempsey invited me to visit him at home in the evening: to take tea and cakes and to meet his wife, at their flat in the Gray's Inn Road. 'I've spoken about you often to my wife,' he said. 'She greatly looks forward to meeting you. She doesn't get about much; she's not awfully strong. I have to make sure she takes care of herself; she's all I have, my dear, we never had children – and we're as much in love as we were when we first married. So you see, I'm very fortunate.'

The Dempseys lived just around the corner from Doughty Street, where Dickens's house was. I discovered a tall, grey, four-storeyed terrace of intimidating gloom: a house from *Little Dorrit*. The Dempsey flat was reached by climbing three flights of steep, narrow stairs through semi-darkness, and proved to be simply a double room with a tiny kitchen and no bathroom. There were two frayed old armchairs of Genoa velvet; a cheap dining-room table; a small, crowded bookshelf; a sagging double bed in a corner half disguised by cushions. The central light was weak and we sat in a brownish gloom, eating our cream cakes and buns and drinking our tea. I guessed that they'd spent more on the cakes than they could afford.

But the Dempseys were vivacious and happy, and plainly pleased to entertain me. Yvette Dempsey was much the same age as her husband, probably in her late sixties: frail and bird-like, with a thin face of faded French prettiness, her pale eyes just discernible behind tinted glasses. Her English was not good; it seemed they spoke French a good deal between themselves.

'He speaks very much about you,' she said. 'He says you will become a real author. That is a brave thing to be. My husband has also written a book, did you know?'

They sat side by side, holding hands in their unperturbed poverty, and I saw that what Mr Dempsey had said was true: they were very much in love with each other. Glancing at a small side table set against the wall, my eye was caught by a drawing in a frame, and when I peered at it, I became embarrassed: it was a sketch of Mr Dempsey I had done myself, on the back of a piece of Hearts of Oak stationery, whiling away time at the table. Mrs Dempsey smiled. 'It is such a good likeness,' she said. 'I had it framed.' But the crookedness and smeared paste told me that they had framed it themselves.

I visited the Dempseys perhaps twice more. Soon afterwards, I resigned from the Hearts of Oak, having found a more exalted and well-paid clerical job in the London office of BHP, the major Australian iron and steel corporation. The old gentleman in the glass office to whom I tendered my resignation surveyed me reproachfully. 'So it's a higher salary,' he said. 'BHP? Never heard of it. You may get more money from these fly-by-night organisations, but in the Hearts of Oak you'd have been secure for life.'

Mr Dempsey seemed very much affected when I left, and told me many times to keep in touch with him; to call on him and his wife again, in the Gray's Inn Road. 'You'll succeed,' he said. 'Never doubt it, my dear. And if you get discouraged, remember: "Be still, be still, my soul; it is but for a season." You will call on us? Don't forget. We'll be waiting. You're like a son to us.'

I promised him that I'd come, and I intended to; but I never did. Derek and Buddy drifted out of my life too, because now I'd found a girl, and had escaped from that London which is the capital of loneliness, where the aged and the lost wander in calm despair. Young, poor and happy, my English girlfriend and I held hands along the Embankment and over Waterloo Bridge; we watched Richard Burton play Iago at the Old Vic; we listened to Hancock's Half Hour on the radio in my bedsitter at night, as the iron, majestic cold of the northern winter closed in, and the pea soupers that Holmes and Watson knew began. We tied handkerchiefs around our noses against the smog; breathing in, we left a yellow stain. But I was not appalled by this winter; it was winter in the city of cities, the grim and gentle old friend I had waited for. I thrilled to its sheer, icy edge, and looked up at the pole star, and discovered what I believed no one had noticed before: that the moon here was upside down. Or rather, I told Patricia, the moon in Australia was upside down; and I now understood why the man in the moon's face, in English nursery books, was shown in pictures to have a mouth like an O. In Australia, the mouth was one of the eyes . . .

But recollection of London happiness is tainted with the

knowledge of how I failed Mr Dempsey. There are omissions that can never be made good, and cheerful little Dempsey and his pretty French wife wait for me still, after thirty-odd years, holding hands in the brown gloom of that tall old terrace in the Gray's Inn Road: that house out of *Little Dorrit* that could not crush their spirits. In a hollow of the heart where the Marshalsea Prison stands, in a London that doesn't exist, old Dempsey waits, and his shade will not release me. Some day, he and I will sell bicycles to the Americans.

# California Dreaming,
# Hermann Hesse and the Great God Pot

I

We seldom see clearly the country through which we're travelling. The topography is only obvious looking backwards; and in California in 1960, all that was certain was that the countryside was new.

My wife and I, just arrived in the United States, sat in a bar in San Francisco watching the Kennedy–Nixon debate on black and white television. We'd been married only a few months, and here we were in America, assailed by the images and sounds of a lifetime of Hollywood films; by America's trumpet-notes of blatant promise and excitement. We had fallen in love with San Francisco, this easy, happy town still haunted by the Beat generation, which had yet to experience the explosion of Flower Power and the drug culture. We'd also fallen for John Kennedy, and we felt a little sorry for dark-jowled Nixon, sweating on his podium, so obviously outclassed by the handsome Irish charmer, and seeming even then to be guilty about something. Rounding a bend in the river of history, racing into a new era, we were mere extras in the crowd; two young foreigners from a quaint, obscure country on the bottom of the world, which Americans then either thought of as 'British', or else were totally vague about.

We had rented a pleasant, shabby apartment on Nob Hill; and our landlord, Mr Harper, an elderly, bald Texan who looked like Henry Miller, was one of the vague ones. Conducting a genial interview with us in his sitting room, he had pulled down a wall map. 'Now let's see. Where are you folks from?'

Australia, we said; and he peered at the map in a bemused, admiring manner. 'Way down there! And did you folks learn the American language to come here?'

We tried to explain our common heritage of English; but he shook his head in delighted blankness.

'Well, I must say you speak our language well. You don't have hardly any brogue at all.'

Sprawled on cushions in the multicoloured dusk at Ken Kesey's parties, in his pretty, wood-shingled, fairy-tale cottage out on Perry Lane, Palo Alto – drunk on cheap Californian wine, or enclosed by the new, dangerous pungency of the weed we all called pot – how could we know that the drug culture was being invented before our eyes? But it was true: with his seductively alarming marijuana joints, his LSD, his nameless pills and mushrooms – a specially-rigged 'psychedelic light' revolving above the hubbub in the cottage's dim ceiling to stain our faces with all the colours of the rainbow, the loudspeakers of his sound system strung in the oak trees outside so that the great, driving voice of Odetta was everywhere – Kesey was one of the drug culture's chief inventors: its future high priest.

Padding with an athlete's quickness in jeans and sneakers among his guests, apparently unaffected by whatever he was on, while others lay comatose in corners, or grinned in a wild cosmos of their own, Ken looked like the champion wrestler he'd once been, and had the wholesome vitality of the Oregon farm-boy he still essentially was – the whites of his pale blue eyes clean; his skin clear. He resembled a much more powerful and muscular Paul Newman, his balding, rope-yellow hair curling on a neck like a bull's. He drew people around him as those who radiate vitality always do: and he conveyed an illicit and chuckling promise. And although that promise revolved about mind-altering chemicals and plants, and the sort of sexual experiment and promiscuity which in 1960 was still somewhat shocking, it had about it a paradoxical air of vigorous adventurousness: the happy, boyish daring of pioneer days. Ken was a profoundly American man. He loved the old Western songs; among his boyhood heroes were figures like Buffalo Bill Cody, and I imagine the Oregon Trail was very near in his consciousness. Drugs and sexual licence were the New Frontier, and as Rosemary and Stephen Vincent Benét said of the old pioneers: 'The cowards never started, and the weak died on the road.' In the end it would be to Kesey's frontier, not John Kennedy's, that the young would flock.

His wife Faye, faintly Slavonic, smiled on us all with the calm enigma of an earth mother. A baby dangled in a cradle hung from a beam, swinging amid the noise; occasionally Ken would give it a kick to keep it swinging. The baby seemed quite happy. Ken wasn't yet famous; *One Flew Over the Cuckoo's Nest*, which he was still writing, while working as a male nurse on the Menlo Park psychiatric ward that provided its setting, wouldn't be published for another twelve months or so. Neither was the lanky, saturnine Texan Larry McMurtry famous yet. He sat in a corner, grinning his cheerfully sardonic grin, scholarly spectacles flashing, long legs outstretched in their jeans and cowboy boots, watching the action. His first novel hadn't yet become the film, *Hud*; and *The Last Picture Show* and *Terms of Endearment* were still far in the future. We were all in our mid or late twenties, most of us enrolled for a year at the Stanford University Writing Center – filled with limitless hopes and a limitless capacity for exhilaration and laughter that swelled around us like a big balloon.

The parties were constant. They were held in the bungalows of Palo Alto around the Stanford campus, or else at my apartment or Larry's, back down the highway in San Francisco. But the ones at the cottage on Perry Lane always held the most glamour. Nearly everyone had a guitar or a banjo, Kesey included. Sometimes we would enter a house to find a dozen or so banjos and guitars tinkling and throbbing at once in the various rooms – usually playing bluegrass, and filling us with a wave of sentimental joy: the old mountain music conjuring up all the exuberance of the vast republic looming outside in the night; all that was electric and generous in America.

The folk revival was only just beginning. We listened then to Odetta and Leadbelly and Woody Guthrie, and the songs we sang were mostly traditional American and British ballads: 'Goodbye, Old Paint'; 'High Barbaree'; 'This Land is Your Land'; 'Five Hundred Miles'; 'This Train is Bound for Glory' . . . We wanted to be professional writers, but what we also frankly wanted was raw fun; and in that year at Stanford, it seldom seemed to stop. It was a simple and euphoric time, a sort of second youth spent as undergraduates by people who were not undergraduates, with little in it that was vicious, and a good deal that was fond and generous. But as the academic year of 1960–61 went on, most of us began to grasp the fact that Ken's fun was serious, and not childish: a sort of secret ideology, leading deeper and deeper into a maze. Enormously likeable, impossible to ignore or forget, Kesey was plainly a leader, a genial guru-figure; but not everyone wanted to go into his maze – whose door, in my imagination at least, was labelled *Derangement.*

It was Gurney Norman who tried Kesey's mushrooms. The rest of us Stanford writers had too strong a sense of self-preservation for that; we stuck to wine and pot, and left mushrooms and LSD trips to the remnants of the Beat generation. But Gurney, an amiable young writer from Kentucky, crew-cut and clean-cut as a character from a 1950s college movie, decided to take the trip. There are people who do not emerge from mushroom trips without permanent mental damage; Gurney survived, but he lost two days, and reported to us on the world he had entered with excited alarm.

'Ah was drivin' down the freeway by mahself, an' suddenly the knobs on the dashboard turned into two big eyes, *starin'* at me. Ah told mahself: "Those ain't eyes, they're knobs on the dashboard"; an' they went back to being knobs again. But pretty soon it got worse, and wouldn't stop. Ah got home, an' this *giant* followed me across the lawn. Ah tell you, a *giant*! Ah don't know *what* it was, an' Ah don't *want* to know! It was tryin' to get into the house! An' then Ah was seeing things all the time. The last two days, Ah don't even know where Ah've *been*! Ah don't want any more of that.'

The Stanford Writing Class of 1960–61 was an unusual one, and I believe is already being seen in the United States as historic, since it included so many writers who made good: Kesey, Larry McMurtry, Peter Beagle, James Baker Hall and the theatrical producer Arvin Brown, to name the most prominent; and it was run in different semesters by the critic and Viking Press editor, Malcolm Cowley, and by the great Irish short-story writer Frank O'Connor. I had won a fellowship to the Writing Center through Melbourne University, and I'd arrived with a very sceptical attitude towards the Writing Class, and the whole concept I thought would be behind it. I was working on my second novel, and was grateful for the time the fellowship gave me to write, since one was only required to attend the class on two afternoons a week; but I didn't believe that creative writing could be formally taught.

However, I was to find that my fears of any serious attempts to do so were largely groundless, and that most of my fellow writers (a number of whom, like me, had already published first novels) shared my views. The Center was really a sort of launching pad for young writers whose promise was already clear; and our afternoons around the long table in our pleasant tutorial room at Stanford proved to be happy, stimulating, and different from what I had expected. I can't truthfully say that I learned a great deal more about my craft in a direct way, although we all perhaps had a little literary self-indulgence nudged out of us; but our sessions really resembled those informal soirées that young writers tend to hold among themselves, reading their work to one another and discussing it – the great difference being that when we read our work-in-progress here, one of the century's most eminent critics passed opinion on it, genially, kindly, but sometimes ruthlessly. And we listened in awe. White-moustached Malcolm Cowley, nodding over his cigar like a benign grandfather to us all, was a legendary figure: the man who had been in Paris with the Lost Generation; who had known and dealt professionally with the giants: Faulkner, Hemingway, Fitzgerald. He would tell us anecdotes about them, and compare our technical problems with theirs, and we glowed with a sense of continuity. It was he who saw the potential of *One Flew Over the Cuckoo's Nest*; Kesey would arrive from the hospital and read us his latest section each week, and Cowley would nod and grin in approval;

ultimately he bought it for Viking, and the rest, as they say, is history.

But the trouble with such soirées, like most group activities that have to do with entertainment, is that the practitioners begin to want an audience reaction – and the one clearly favourable reaction to a literary reading is laughter in the right places. All other reactions are silent; and one soon finds silence inadequate and even ambiguous. So we began to read our funny bits to the class in preference to any others; and measured on the laughter-indicator, the most successful story of the year was one by Jim Hall called 'The Turd in the Swimming Pool'. I don't think it had the highest literary merit, but it certainly got the most laughs. High seriousness in such a situation is hard to maintain after a time, since the seriousness of young writers easily becomes self-admiring; and in the end I remained convinced that writing isn't really a group sport.

The trouble began in the second half of the academic year, under Frank O'Connor. For a time, the relationship was happy; although a cultural gap existed between O'Connor and the Americans, as it sometimes did for me. As legendary in his way as Malcolm Cowley, and a very proud man, O'Connor was a little testy in his old age, with not long to live, and plainly critical of the new values being born in America in 1961. In a number of ways during discussion, it became evident that he and I, an Irishman and an Australian of different ages, some-how came from the same background, the same value-system, in contrast with the Americans – and despite my warm good fellowship with these young men and women of my own age, many of whom were becoming real friends, there was an area in which Frank O'Connor and I were foreigners to them, and not to each other. As we agreed on some moral or literary point to which the rest of the table objected, O'Connor's eyes and mine would meet in mutual support or amused bafflement. The occasion on which this happened with most clarity was when one of the class read us a story he had written in the first person about a paedophile who had raped and then killed a small girl.

This was the period when American expert and popular concern was coming to focus largely on the criminal, not the victim, in the way that has since had such profound legal and social consequences throughout the West. The criminal needed all our sympathy and understanding; if possible, we should identify with him; and the story took this proposition to somewhat unusual lengths. The paedophile–murderer had committed his crime in a deserted, beautiful spot – as I recall, in the long grass beside a river – and told from his point of view, it all seemed very understandable and natural, or was meant to. 'You don't understand,' he said (or words to that effect). 'It was cool and beautiful down there.'

When the author had finished, there was near unanimous agreement around the table that a powerful effect had been created, and that the mind of the killer had been sympathetically entered. But Frank O'Connor and I sat staring at each other in silence from opposite ends of the table. His face expressed an incredulous distaste; and I decided to voice the thought we both knew we were sharing.

'But what about the little girl?'

There was a surprised silence.

'That's right,' O'Connor said. 'What about the murdered child? And her parents? What thought does your story give to them?'

They stared; we were speaking a language that was not only unfashionable; it was barely understood.

Old O'Connor got more and more testy as the year went on, and less popular with the class. He began to insist more and more on the craft of good, plain storytelling, and to dismiss as pretentious anything more artistically ambitious. He was particularly scathing towards a humourless, somewhat amateurish writer who had produced huge purple passages about his great mother the sea.

'Give up all this bloody symbolism, for Christ's sake,' O'Connor scolded. 'Try to tell a decent *story*, man, and have done with it.'

'But sir,' the victim protested, 'James Joyce used symbolism.'

O'Connor gave him his most withering stare. 'My dear fellow,' he said, 'Joyce was a don. You are *not*.'

He ended by demanding that the short-story writers submit plotlines to him. If he approved, they could go ahead; if not, the story should be abandoned. This caused a rebellion. The whole class, with Larry McMurtry as its spokesman, informed him that such a prescriptive method of dealing with our work was unacceptable, and inhibited our creative freedom. O'Connor, proud and angry, told us that he had been asked here to teach us the craft of the story, of which he was an acknowledged master, and that this was what he was trying to do. But we remained implacable; we could not accept such a method as he was proposing.

He appealed to me, his ally: didn't I think his methods reasonable?

No, I said, I didn't believe writing could actually be taught like that. I probably qualified what I said; but it was tactless, and I'm still ashamed to recall the pain in his face.

After a week, realising how much we had hurt him, we all apologised. He eventually became quite friendly again with most of the others, but me he never forgave. I was his Judas.

It was true, I suppose. O'Connor was a Victorian, essentially; and despite the gap in our ages, so in some ways was I. We are formed by our grandparents as well as our parents, and mine were Victorians. As well as that, I came from a country where many Victorian values were still preserved in amber. This made Ken Kesey not just startling to me, but disturbing.

It was during one of the parties in our Nob Hill apartment that Kesey introduced my wife and me to pot smoking. Marijuana was still dangerous then, police surveillance being seriously carried out – so it was with a thrill of risk as well as unease that we passed through the door into the maze.

It must have been good-quality stuff. At one stage, Ken sat me down at a table and spread out handfuls of peppermints in even amounts in front of himself and me. These were little men, he said, and he and I were going to fight a battle. After a time, in spite of my ability to retain some grip on reality, I began actually to believe in the campaign and these little men, and grew hilarious about them, aware that much of it had to do with Ken's powers of suggestion. Later we went to a night-time fun fair and rode the roller coaster: we were truly flying, and our bodies roared with delight and terror. But eventually I became somewhat alarmed at being inside a bubble I couldn't escape, and I began to understand the term 'spaced out'. There was a space at the front of my brain, and I found this an alarming phenomenon.

Kesey's theories on creativity and drug-taking, expounded with proselytising intensity, were not novel to me. He and his life style were, but not the theories – which derived from familiar sources such as Rimbaud, Aldous Huxley and

Hermann Hesse. At the age of twenty-eight, I'd already become sceptical of these post-Romantic notions of the artist as divine madman; and I began to have debates with Kesey that grew more and more hard-line. He was always good-humoured and polite, but an undertone of exasperation sometimes crept in. Plainly, I was a stubborn square, but I had to be tolerated: I was a visitor from an old-fashioned country, after all, and it would take time to persuade me. Our arguments continued, often with an audience of friends.

Didn't I see, he said, that drugs opened doors to unknown levels of vision, and that if I wrote my work while taking them, I would produce insights and revelations I could never otherwise have?

No, I said, there was no short cut to vision for a writer. The vision had to be already in us; and drugs wouldn't discover anything that wasn't already there: they would only turn it into static. Nor could we give up the mind's control, since no worthwhile art could be produced where the intellect was crippled, where a space had entered the mind. I was opposed to that space.

It was the old clash of Dionysian and Apollonian; in the end, we had to agree to disagree. Soon, very soon, Ken would have so many disciples that a few Jeremiahs like me couldn't matter; by the time he and his Merry Pranksters drove their famous bus across America, Kesey would be a powerful figure: 'the Chief'. And power, I suppose, was what the bus trip and the drug trips were largely about.

Larry McMurtry, shrewd and phlegmatic in the Texan style, didn't debate with Ken; but I noticed he didn't use marijuana much either. Like many writers, he was a watcher, not a participant; and like me, he didn't much care to lose control.

We had that in common, and much else besides, and we became firm friends. Larry and his wife Jo, like my wife and me, preferred to live in San Francisco rather than Palo Alto; and every Wednesday and Friday Larry would give me a lift in his long black Ford out to the Stanford writing class. On those thirty-mile rides along the Bayshore Freeway, he and I discovered how much a boyhood on a ranch in West Texas and one spent largely in rural Tasmania had in common. Living on my uncle's farm in the Derwent Valley, I had grown up with the same Country and Western songs as Larry had; we shared the same favourites, and we tuned in on the car radio to a C & W station, listening contentedly to Hank Snow, Kitty Wells and Roy Acuff as a background to our talk.

I learned a lot about America from Larry on those rides. A son and grandson of cattle ranchers, he was deeply fond of his country, across which he drove continually, carried perhaps by that same nomadic instinct which had taken so many members of the McMurtry clan on the great nineteenth-century cattle drives. Endlessly fascinated by America's variety and vitality, Larry nevertheless admitted that a sort of madness was abroad lately, expressing itself in senseless violence and the new experiments with drugs.

'Anything's possible in this country,' he told me. 'Just about anything. You can have most anything you want and *do* most anything you want – in theory. But of course not everyone succeeds. And infinite possibilities can be plenty destructive – they drive some folks crazy. There's a new craziness and dangerousness that folks like my parents just don't know about.'

Looking at the country whirring by outside the window, I believed I understood what he meant. Beyond the great, multilayered freeway, with its myriad overpasses and endless flashing lines of traffic, out beyond the avenues of advertising billboards, there were level vistas that seemed to hum with promise: but of what? There was a baffling quality about the Californian distance: electric pylons stepped into bayside mist; the earth was scarred red by bulldozers preparing new housing developments; activity and life were everywhere; and yet the satellite towns strung out along the peninsula had a two-dimensional, doubtful quality, like film sets made from plaster and plywood; they were not very real, and seemed half lost in the huge, coastal landscape which itself had the look of a mirage. Its grass was the grey-green of faded paint; its rust-and-blue distances seemed ready to float into some other dimension. It was the freeway alone, US 101, that was real, and to be in contact with the spirit of this land it was necessary to be moving, necessary to be here inside the car, locked in the traffic stream on the silver-grey highway, going at high speed. And this was what Kesey had understood. There was a necessity here to escape, to puncture a hole in reality, since reality didn't satisfy; reality itself wasn't real enough. You had to go on a trip to get relief: any trip. The American landscape itself was pregnant with this demand; or had it been infected with the impossible longings of those who'd built on it with such frantic energy? Who could say?

In seven years' time, a far less amiable and very different Chief than Kesey would wander through these bland Californian vacancies, followed by more sinister disciples.

Ex-convict Charlie Manson would feed his youthful followers on a similar diet of drugs, free love, music and dreams: but the dreams would have a new and terrifying dimension. To his 'family' of dissociated middle-class girls and psychotic, vagrant men, Charlie was 'love'; Charlie was the ultimate seer, a new sort of Christ, who was going to take them eventually down a tunnel that only he knew about in Death Valley, which reached to the centre of the earth: what they significantly called 'the bottomless pit', from where they would rule a fragmented world. Power and destruction: this was the great trip now; and the Manson family, like the Merry Pranksters, were filled with glee at deriding the straight world. When Manson's followers butchered the pregnant Sharon Tate and their other victims, they were giggling like children. They were doing 'the Devil's work', they said; for Charlie, they would do anything. And somehow, looking back on those Californian landscapes of 1961, remembering the parties on Perry Lane and the maddening hum of impossible promise, I think I'm able to half understand how the horrors happened.

Did Timothy Leary and Ken Kesey create Charlie Manson? Surely not. But in searching for new dimensions of freedom, for unnatural beauty born out of chemicals, for experience without limits, they helped in the end to create a different ethos perhaps from the one they bargained for. Taking the works of Hermann Hesse as Holy Writ, they had rejected the dull, exterior world altogether, and had led their enthusiasts off on an interior journey: what Leary, in his famous essay on Hesse called 'a psychedelic journey' – deep inside the self. But the American dream, which required instant action, was alive and well; and to supply instant revelation, drugs and magic mushrooms were at hand, opening the doors immediately, without the tedium of meditation. The Magic Theatre of *Steppenwolf* was theirs; everyone would gain admittance (this being democracy) and instant art and literature would flow forth too. Everyone would be an artist, through the good offices of the Great God Pot. This message was what so impressed the Beatles – in whose songs Charlie Manson heard special and terrible meanings. This was the West Coast's most influential contribution to the West.

Two decades on, it all seems curiously innocent: harmlessly silly and exuberant. Those thousands of young men and women dying of overdosing in the streets and public toilets of the West's great cities: are they Ken Kesey's children? Timothy Leary's? John Lennon's? Surely not. Perhaps they're the grandchildren of Hermann Hesse.

2

In the sixties and seventies, no flower child or counter-culture person was complete without a copy of *Steppenwolf* in his or her rough leather handbag. There were Hermann Hesse rock groups, Hermann Hesse nightclubs, Hermann Hesse T-shirts; even Hermann Hesse comic books. Hesse had become a literary man for the non-literary; even for the semi-literate. The counter-culture of America – a country he despised, and said would never read his books – had made him into a prophet, and then into an industry.

For the literary minded of an earlier generation, this was a puzzling phenomenon, leading to false expectations. In apartments scented with marijuana, in buses or on aeroplanes, falling into conversation with the owner of a paperback *Narziss and Goldmund* or *Siddhartha*, I would wait for the revelation of a refined literary taste. My companion was at grips with a remorselessly spiritual German author of a somewhat elite cast of mind, whose long career had begun with the century. An interest in Thomas Mann as well seemed likely. But no; other serious novels of the period were not making a comeback, and it soon became plain that Hesse was a talisman: he had to be imbibed like a joint of marijuana to indicate membership of the movement. No other interest in the novel was necessary, except for a reading of Ken Kesey – at the mention of whose name the eyes of the flower child would light up.

In an interesting and revealing biography published some years ago, *Hermann Hesse, Pilgrim of Crisis*, Dr Ralph Freedman has analysed with some thoroughness what it was that America found in Hesse. The roots of the revival, he points out, can be traced to Colin Wilson's 1956 book, *The Outsider*, which presented Hesse as a symbolic outsider-figure in the era that had produced those other outsiders, the Beat generation. Then Timothy Leary claimed *Steppenwolf* in particular as a bible and guide for the drug culture of the sixties, and the author of *Siddhartha* was seen as a mystic of the East – just when the youth of the West were turning east in their thousands. But Dr Freedman remarks that the West Coast found things in Hesse that Hesse would not have imagined – and he makes the amusing point that Hesse's acceptability was partly possible because 'translation blurred the distinct upper-middle-class flavour of the original language'. The counter-culture created a new Hermann Hesse, he says. But earlier vogues for Hesse had appeared in Europe among the young, dating back to the period before World War I; Hesse, through-out his very long writing life, was a public artist who went through a series of personal crises each of which uncannily expressed the crises of our age. This was why he so often became a mentor and cult figure to the young. And what he was writing throughout was a single creative autobiography.

Hesse began as a nature writer, his first successful novel, *Peter Camenzind* (1904), being a hymn to artistic friendship and life in the outdoors, away from corrupting cities. It made an impact on a young generation in Germany wanting to reject the rise of a new, technocratic society. Then came World War I, during which Hesse withdrew to Switzerland, and became a Swiss citizen – not rejecting his German identity nor opposing the war directly, but unable to enthuse about it. Unfit for military service, he was able to remain aloof, and spoke out against nationalism, drawing attacks from his native land. At forty, he published *Demian*, which brought him fame among a new generation affected by the lost war. They responded to its mystique of the individual self as the sole source of value. *Demian* rejects the conventional Christian morality in which Hesse was reared, his parents having been devout Pietists and his maternal grandfather having been a missionary in India – a fact which helped to awaken Hesse's romantic interest in the East.

A third crisis, and a third major success, came with World War II. Once again Hesse remained in Switzerland, detached from the conflict; but he still could not renounce his German roots, nor look with equanimity on the threatened loss of his German readership and royalties. The Nazis detested and vilified him, but did not ban him, and he took pleasure in the fact that German soldiers carried his books into battle. But he was denounced in Germany as a traitor – only to be attacked at the end of the war for his comfortable non-involvement. This caused him much distress – alleviated by the success of *The Glass Bead Game* which won him the Nobel Prize after the war.

All these waves in Hesse's career had one thing in common: they came at moments of psychological, social and cultural crisis. Hesse's life was marked by a series of breakdowns: mental and physical. He was plagued by eye trouble, headaches

and intestinal disorders. He had three marriages. He constantly entered spas for cures, and was one of the first writers to be
psychoanalysed, his fruitful friendship with Jung resulting in
the use of Jung's ideas in his novels. A typical Cancerian, he
survived all his trials while complaining bitterly to the end;
and the ultimate impression left by a perusal of his life is
one of indomitable self-centredness, as well as of the self-
preservation necessary to an artist. While his first wife, Mia (who
finally had a complete mental collapse), remained at home,
Hesse went on tours to Italy and elsewhere with his friends,
and on the health cures that were plainly an escape. In a letter
in 1912 he boasted that his physician had relieved him of his
responsibilities, and that a wealthy friend was paying his bills.

The other dominant impression created both by an exam-
ination of Hesse's career and a concentrated reading of his
novels is one of very narrow limits; of a few constant preoccupations, over that long creative life, which do not seem to
have led out into any real uplands. Despite Hesse's great ability
to capture intense spiritual experience, and his lyrical evoca-
tions of the discovery of love and the physical world, there is an
abstract quality about his writing, so that it reads like summary
rather than full creation: we are locked inside the author's
mind, and the world and other people do not really come alive
as they do in the greatest novels. Dr Freedman, in one passage
in his biography, tacitly recognises this, although he doesn't
condemn it:

There was no real India in *Siddhartha*; there was no real
Basel and Zürich of the twenties in *Steppenwolf.* There was
only a dream and a sermon spoken by a mythical persona,
Hermann Hesse.

Hesse's pilgrimage seems to have gone in a circle; and reading Dr Freedman's account of his life brought me to a sudden understanding of why it is that the novels have always had a peculiar and paradoxical effect on me. Beginning each one with renewed admiration for the quality of the writing, and with a sense of expectancy, I would always end with a feeling of diminishment, of dissatisfaction. The biography demonstrates that all these works of fiction reproduce Hesse's own spiritual evolution, repeated in many variations; but the preoccupations remain the same, from youth into age. One does not gain a sense, reading about Hesse's life, of spiritual growth. And perhaps this accounts for the curious airlessness in the novels, which create a sense of oppressiveness rather than release, like a set of boxes in which one is trapped.

I'm sure this is the opposite of what Hesse intended, and it plainly isn't the way Dr Freedman sees his work. In fact, he maintains that Hesse has given 'sustenance and guidance' to an entire culture. This is a statement worth examining. How nourishing has that 'sustenance' been, and what sort of meat was it?

Hesse in his childhood was constantly divided between the 'two worlds' he describes so brilliantly in *Demian*: the world of light, equated with his home and parents; and the world of dark – of outsiders, of hostile but alluring powers. He was a prey to much fear and depression in childhood, and the Pietist version of Christianity seems to have been almost entirely negative in its effect on him. Although his parents were just and kind, and although he was deeply attached to them both, at fifteen he became uncontrollable, and was regarded as mentally disturbed. He was put in the care of a clergyman, Blumhardt, who specialised in exorcism. When Hesse suffered disappointment over his infatuation with a girl, he attempted suicide; and Blumhardt suggested he was possessed by evil spirits. He was sent for some months to Stetten, an institution for retarded and epileptic children. A little later he was put in the happier Basel Mission school, and ultimately came home again. He resented his father for what had happened, and his letters home are a mixture of appeals and defiance. He tells his parents that 'Your God ... doesn't interest me'; and goes on: 'Now you'll immediately serve up Jesus and God, but I don't know them; still I'd like to say to someone: "Help, help me." But there'd have to be someone who would ... put me into a different world.'

This cry for help came from a boy who was actually the object of love and concern; yet no evidence exists to show that Hesse was actually mentally ill. Dr Freedman doesn't discuss the clergyman's suggestion of diabolic possession – probably assuming, such being the fashion of our time, that it is not deserving of serious consideration. But perhaps, in some form, it should be considered. There is a level at which the idea of demonic possession can make sense to minds not receptive to the supernatural – even if it is only seen as a metaphor to describe the plight of certain obsessed spirits.

Hesse's breakdown led to attempts at flight, drinking bouts, and final failure at school, despite his evident intellect; so that when he left, it was to become a bookshop assistant, while his friends went to university. He went on writing loving letters to his parents from his new job, and this involvement continued until their deaths. How is one to account for such a collapse in a sheltered boy – a collapse so violent that his parents could not cope with it? He himself called it 'that old devil feeling', and Parson Schall spoke of 'moral insanity'.

And the child was father to the man. All his writing searches for that 'different world' for which he cried out; and in almost all his novels, commencing with *Demian* (Demon) there appears an individual who is to show him that world, who is to be his spiritual guide, and initiate him into mysteries. But they are not mysteries that involve deeper knowledge of God. What then, are these mysteries? What is a novel like *Demian* really saying? Hesse is deliberately ambiguous, but there are clues.

From the time of the idealised Max Demian's appearance as a schoolboy, until his sentimentally drawn death scene on the battlefield, he is quite obviously a witch-figure, able to summon up secret powers to protect Hesse–Sinclair from a bully, and to watch his progress even when they are physically separated. His conversion of the admiring Sinclair begins when he tells him that Cain, in the Old Testament, was not really evil, whether he slew his brother or not, but a 'fine fellow', an archetypal strong man of whom weaklings were afraid: hence the 'mark of Cain' on his brow.

What this is all about is power: the power to master both others and one's own destiny that is always the aim of witch-craft: the power to rise above supposedly ordinary notions of good and evil. There is an echo, of course, of Nietzsche's *Übermensch*; but there is more. Demian speaks of a God called Abraxas, who reconciles the godly and satanic: who is in fact both God and the Devil.

A similar gospel was preached in the deserts of California by Charles Manson: a seedy and appalling Max Demian for the 1960s. That Manson and his fanatical 'family' were conscious satanists has been well established by their prosecutor, Vincent Bugliosi; there were connections with a satanic cult called the Process – which linked Jehovah, Lucifer, Satan and Christ. Manson simplified this: he himself, he said, was both Satan and Christ. His disciples believed it completely, and his methods of control were based on fear, which he saw as a beneficial tool. Pixie-faced little Susan Atkins, the most terrible of his disciples, who disembowelled Sharon Tate and elatedly tasted her blood having laughed at her pleas for mercy, had this to say about the man who was her God: 'He represented a Jesus Christ-like person to me.' Asked if she saw Charlie as evil, she replied: 'Looking at him through your eyes, I would say yes. Looking at him through my eyes he is as good as he is evil, he is as evil as he is good.'

For his murderous girl disciples, Charlie was 'complete love' – replacing parents, replacing the normal world with a world of his own creation, in which the killing of 'pigs' – the normal people the 'family' loathed – was a duty and a joy. In jail, disciple Sandra Good boasted: 'I've finally reached the point where I can kill my parents.'

Again, one is reminded of *Demian*. Exulting in the truths Demian has revealed, Sinclair says:

> I had suddenly seen through his world of light and wisdom! Indeed I myself who was Cain . . . because of my wickedness and misfortune . . . stood higher than my father, higher than the pious and righteous.

It is much the same message, years on, at the end of *Steppenwolf* – this time delivered by Pablo, another magus, in his Magic Theatre. Hesse's latest persona, Haller, sees himself in a mirror: his many selves, broken into fragments. *Steppenwolf* is a fascinating work, with the compulsion and mystery of a great fairy story; but at the end, this is all there is: the pieces of Haller–Hesse, fragmented after his inward journey, surrounded by semi-illusory figures who have simply been there to assist him in this process. They are not people of flesh and blood, but shadows, as in infancy, who are there to help in the discovery of self: a self which must take whatever course will give it satisfaction, without heed to received moral laws. And yet this is the work of a man of fifty.

The 'inward journey' proclaimed as one of healing by Hesse did not bring him peace or joy, and his life was one of constant misery, physical and mental. He promised to hang himself at fifty, but changed his mind. His dedication and staying-power must command admiration; but in the end, one doesn't feel that this was the progress of a great soul. Acquaintance with the lives of Tolstoy and Dostoevsky – near-contemporaries, and writers with a similar preoccupation with spiritual growth – does create such a feeling, despite all their inconsistencies, torments and follies. The inward journey of Hesse led to psychic claustrophobia, while the ethic that the two Russians continued to embrace led to a focusing outwards, and a sort of exaltation. Turning outwards towards others, believing that the sufferings of others concerned them, they created living and pulsating people, for whom we can fervently care. No such figures appear on Hesse's journeys.

There is a pattern in everything, and that the ego-centred West adopted Hesse as a mentor in the sixties was a sure indicator of its spiritual situation. The exploration of the ego, seen then as the key to wisdom, does not seem to have brought the enlightenment or happiness it was supposed to do. Perhaps Hell is not other people, but the unrelieved contemplation of the self.

# The Last Novelist

As the Jazz Age dwindles into legendary remoteness, the legend of F. Scott Fitzgerald grows larger, and the biographies and studies flow on, with no sign of ceasing.

Like all true legends, Fitzgerald's has a mystery at its heart: that of achieved perfection, which people recognise instinctively in literature, even if they can't define it. Fitzgerald was reaching for it in all his novels – and in one of them, *The Great Gatsby*, he gave us one of the most perfect and beautiful things in all fiction. It is this beauty of perfection, I believe, that accounts for the unusual affection in which *Gatsby* is held by so many people; and to some extent it explains the endless interest in Fitzgerald himself. This, and the fact that more than most writers, he exemplifies in his life perfection's paradox: that the perfection came out of heartbreak, folly and mess utterly at odds with the serenity of his art.

Another source of fascination is that Fitzgerald experienced in his short life the extremities of fame and failure – beginning as the handsome, carefree poet–prince, the voice of the 1920s, and ending as an alcoholic screenwriter in the Hollywood of the late thirties, his books all but out of print, his wife Zelda in a mental home. He is pictured in a letter by John O'Hara as 'a prematurely old, little man haunting bookstores'. He was forty-four when a heart attack killed him.

Matthew J. Bruccoli, Professor of English at the University of South Carolina, has devoted himself to a study of Fitzgerald's life and works over thirty years: and that amounts to a grand passion. His is possibly the most thoroughly documented and detailed life yet written, and has a plain dispassionateness that inspires confidence. It spares us nothing of the alcoholic odyssey of waste and foolishness that could make one weep; yet it shows us a man the essentials of whose character were generosity and courage: a man whom Professor Bruccoli calls a flawed hero. The battered old term seems not inappropriate, applied to Fitzgerald. He comes into focus now as both an Irish drunk and a genius, a Bohemian and a man of Victorian rectitude, dedicated to the Keatsian ideal of beauty, with literature his pole star. Ernest Hemingway, in one of his typically cruel and patronising letters to Fitzgerald, said: 'You see, Bo, you're not a tragic character.' But in fact, he was. He struggled with his fate to the end, crippled by a single weakness, tormented by a love that ruined his life; but never defeated.

Biographies of Scott Fitzgerald must inevitably be biographies of Zelda as well. He never ceased to love her, though Hemingway insisted that she was destroying his talent and his ability to work; and there can be little doubt that she did much to wreck his peace, driven by some terrible need to compete with him: a fear of being overshadowed which was negative in its effects. But it wasn't that simple; it never is. Professor Bruccoli puts it well:

> ... It is folly to assign blame to either partner. They conspired in a dangerous game for which only they knew the rules.

When that game began, the world was an endless party; and theirs was one of the great tragic loves, in the romantic style that was already going out of fashion. One of the most heart-

rending documents quoted in Bruccoli's book is the transcript
of a discussion between the Fitzgeralds and Zelda's psychiatrist. They rail and tear at each other; they accuse, and then
this moment occurs:

> Zelda: What is our marriage anyway? It has been nothing but
> a long battle ever since I can remember.
> Fitzgerald: I don't know about that. We were about the most
> envied couple in 1921 in America.
> Zelda: I guess so. We were awfully good showmen.
> Fitzgerald: We were awfully happy . . .

Fitzgerald was faithful to her through everything, until her
descent into insanity finally ended all hope; and he was still
writing to her in her mental home every week, in the year that
he died. He was a devoted father to their daughter, spending
much of what he earned on her education, writing letters to her
at Vassar that glow with a sedate and anxious love. It was hard
for him to provide for Scottie as unstintingly as he did, since the
man who had produced some of the finest work in American
literature was now seen as a pathetic has-been, and was being
humiliated by the half-literate bullies who ran the film industry. He could no longer turn out the hack magazine stories that
had kept him and Zelda in their extravagant lifestyle, and on
which he had wasted so much creative energy. His publishers
and agent refused him any more advances. And yet, at this
time, he was producing a novel which, had death not halted it,
would very likely have been his best: *The Last Tycoon*.

In this fact is his whole tragedy and triumph as an artist: that
he was rising above all his exhaustion and despair, and that the
talent which had produced *The Great Gatsby* burned as pure as
ever.

In his notes for *The Last Tycoon*, he wrote: 'I am the last of the novelists for a long time now.' Professor Bruccoli makes some illuminating comments on this. The sense of 'lastness', he says, permeates much of Fitzgerald's work: he saw himself as a vanishing type, since the radical politics of the thirties and the impending war were sweeping away the dream of endless possibilities that had inspired his work: the dream of the twenties. Fitzgerald had seen this not just as the American dream but as the human dream; and the hope of it had died in him.

2

The Hemingways were in Paris, and when Hemingway heard that the Fitzgeralds were definitely coming, he instructed Perkins* not to give Fitzgerald his address. Scott got him thrown out of one Paris apartment by fighting with the landlord, pissing on the porch, and trying to break down the door at 3 or 4 a.m. Ernest wants to see Scott in public places but doesn't want him in his apartment. The news that Scott is coming to Paris gives Ernest the horrors . . .

Hemingway occupied his non-writing time with sport, and made it appear that hunting and fishing were related to his aesthetic. He had the ability to make everything he did seem to have something to do with literature. Hemingway radiated confidence. Fitzgerald became identified with defeat – largely through his own public statements. A shrewd careerist would not have published the 'Crack-Up' essays. Hemingway attributed Fitzgerald's public humiliations to a love of defeat.

* Maxwell Perkins, Hemingway's and Fitzgerald's editor.

These two quotations come from another work by Professor Bruccoli: *Scott and Ernest – the Authority of Failure and the Authority of Success*, which is a study of the two writers as revealed through their correspondence and friendship with each other. But as the passages demonstrate, friendship may not be quite the right term to apply to the relationship.

The account is plain, often comical and seems at first to have a flavour of cynicism. But slowly one becomes aware that it is imbued with real charity and respect – especially where Fitzgerald is concerned. And the final result is affecting. It's also absorbing, since however their work comes to be regarded by some future epoch, the effect of the pair on anyone involved with prose fiction in the twentieth century would be hard to deny. The personal legends, interwoven with their work, continue to have a haunting flavour, absent from the personal backgrounds of most current writers. Bruccoli comments that Hemingway 'became his own greatest creation' – and adds that a documentary study will 'enlarge our understanding of these geniuses – especially of Hemingway'.

This is rather a sly comment; because Professor Bruccoli's research puts some terrible dents in the Hemingway myth. True, Bruccoli says that 'there is no need to aggrandize either F. Scott Fitzgerald or Ernest Hemingway at the other's expense. Their works will endure for as long as books are read – which is all that really mattered to them.' But whether he has set out to do so or not, he has ended by nailing Hemingway down, with little need for authorial comment, as a self-seeking egotist. Fitzgerald, by contrast – and despite his alcoholism, self-pity and self-destructiveness – emerges as a very attractive human being: generous, morally honest, and utterly without the mean competitiveness that mars so many writers, and which distorted Hemingway in particular. All this makes the waste of so much of Fitzgerald's life and talent all the more poignant, whatever its farcical overtones. Yes, he did it to himself (as far as we choose to do anything catastrophic to ourselves); yet one is brought into contact through these letters with a refined spirit that could not be coarsened, and which somehow seems more European than American. But you have to be born a European, you cannot become one – and this may have been just another of the tensions that tormented Fitzgerald so much.

*The Great Gatsby* will surely endure as long as novels are read; and *Tender is the Night* seems likely to do the same, resonant as it is with a tragic and subtle vision; echoing with a whole, lost life. But whether Hemingway's work will continue to impress and delight readers in the same way I begin to doubt. Like many other writers, I have been influenced and deeply impressed by what Hemingway did with prose in *The First Forty-Nine*, *The Sun Also Rises* and *A Farewell to Arms*: but after that comes the work that grows worse and worse, and finally just embarrassing. And even through the best of Hemingway's works run the fatal seams of falsity, of cruelty, of narcissistic posturing, and of a sort of profound spiritual ill-health. It is therefore choicely ironical to discover that the relationship was one where from the very beginning, Hemingway was the great writer–hero and Fitzgerald the hero-worshipper; Hemingway the genius–success and Fitzgerald the poor drunken failure – to some extent in his own eyes, and entirely so in Hemingway's, who described him contemptuously as 'an Irish rummy'.

Hemingway's judgements on Fitzgerald in various letters to other people are both contradictory and revealing. They do more to betray Hemingway's neurotic inconsistencies than to damage Fitzgerald. In 1951, over ten years after Fitzgerald's death, Hemingway was writing to Malcolm Cowley:

> As you know Scott was one of the worst writers who ever wrote prose . . . He got balled up inventing from mixtures of opposites in people instead of inventing from his knowledge of people themselves . . .

But in a previous letter to Cowley, Hemingway had written: '*Gatsby* is good and *Tender is the Night* is really excellent.' There is a sad irony about this tribute to *Tender is the Night* in particular, since he had never had the generosity to praise the work to Fitzgerald in the latter's lifetime, and in fact tore it to pieces. Fitzgerald desperately needed Hemingway's approval; he had given Hemingway not only endless praise and practical help throughout their acquaintanceship, but the recommendations that had virtually launched Hemingway as a writer. In the time when Fitzgerald was fabulously successful, the golden boy, the prophet of the Jazz Age, Hemingway was unknown; and in his first letter mentioning Hemingway, written from Paris to Scribner's editor Maxwell Perkins in 1924 (and displaying his permanent inability to spell), Fitzgerald said:

> This is to tell you about a young man named Ernest Hemmingway . . . I'd look him up right away. He's the real thing.

From that point until his death, he never ceased to praise Hemingway's work directly to Hemingway himself and to others. When he criticised, the criticism was all constructive, and of the most valuable kind one writer can give another – saving him from the self-indulgence of his weak passages, while pointing out to him where his strengths lay. It is deeply interesting, in fact, to see to what degree Fitzgerald was a self-appointed editor of Hemingway's early work – particularly *The Sun Also Rises* and *A Farewell to Arms*, where his closely reasoned pleas for cuts and changes in regard to certain passages saved Hemingway from the sort of descents into bathos and sheer ineptitude he would make later. Hemingway resented these criticisms, acted on them nevertheless – and then pretty clearly resented having done so.

The difference between them that emerges in these letters is that Fitzgerald truly loved the craft of writing, literature itself being more important to him than the writer who was its instrument, or than anything else; while for Hemingway, it was always a sports arena, where Big Daddy had to be best, and where he made it on his own. Everyone else was a competitor. He did not make it on his own, of course – no one does – but he wanted to pretend so; and Bruccoli suggests that 'Hemingway had a compulsion to declare his independence from . . . writers who could be said to have helped him.' He broke with Sherwood Anderson, Gertrude Stein, John Dos Passos, Ford Madox Ford and a long list of other literary friends, all of whom helped to set him on his way. Scott Fitzgerald stayed the course – although in the end they ceased to meet – because he was apparently endlessly prepared to put up with Hemingway's contemptuous ill-treatment.

The sad truth is that while Hemingway earned more and more money from each novel, Fitzgerald earned less and less from his, despite the fact that his novels got better and better. The great financial rewards he earned were from his callow early novels, and above all from his commercial short stories. The tragic irony of his situation, as it unfolds here, is that it was with *Gatsby*, his masterpiece, that his worldly success began to falter, and that his own self-doubts began: he was to suffer a wound over *Gatsby* from which he would never quite recover. That novel did not sell well, by the standards of the day, and it received a hostile review from Gilbert Seldes which appears to have troubled Fitzgerald, and which Hemingway always insisted had 'blocked' him. It was thus with intense concern for its reception that Fitzgerald published *Tender is the Night* in 1934 – the novel to which he gave his greatest efforts, and which he had struggled to complete over many years, dogged by his drinking and by the appalling relationship with Zelda. It is painfully clear from these letters how much Hemingway's response mattered in particular; receiving none, Fitzgerald wrote:

> Did you like the book? For God's sake drop me a line and tell me one way or the other. You can't hurt my feelings . . .

In reply, he received a three-page typed letter of entirely negative criticism, telling him that although he could write better than anyone else, *Tender* was faked, and that he had dried up as a writer. Hemingway urged him to continue writing, however, and added in a note on the envelope that he had not mentioned the parts of the novel he liked, because Scott would know which parts were good.

Fitzgerald's answer to this deadly missile is admirable in its calm humility and good humour, and is painful to read. It also contains some of Fitzgerald's most interesting and direct statements of his theories of fiction, and refers to Joseph Conrad's renowned and seminal essay, the preface to *The Nigger of the Narcissus*. It makes clear that Fitzgerald and Hemingway were consciously Conrad's heirs in striving to forge a new and higher form of fiction, as highly wrought as poetry or music:

> The theory back of it I got from Conrad's preface to *The Nigger*, that the purpose of a work of fiction is to appeal to the lingering after-effects in the reader's mind . . .

It is only fair to point out that Bruccoli sees Hemingway, on the evidence of these letters, as having been a good friend to Fitzgerald until 1936. But the relationship was always lop-sided, and the unctuous condescension on Hemingway's side always shows, even in the early days. It shows too in *A Moveable Feast*. Recalling his first reading of *Gatsby*, Hemingway declares:

> When I had finished the book I knew that no matter what Scott did nor how he behaved, I must know it was like a sickness and be of any help I could to him and try to be a good friend.

Through the years, he remained the tough, masterful hero and Fitzgerald the hero-worshipper – until, as Hemingway's star rose and Fitzgerald's waned, Fitzgerald was moved to write in his notebook: 'I talk with the authority of failure – Ernest with the authority of success. We could never sit across the table again.' Hemingway spoke of Fitzgerald's 'cheap Irish love of defeat', despising him for his alcoholism and his loyalty to Zelda, whom Hemingway saw as the main cause of Fitz-gerald's destruction. No doubt there was a good deal of truth in this, and no doubt Fitzgerald was impossible and masochistic. But his decency shines through, and the man who called him – among other things – a liar, did so from a very unsound personal base, considering Hemingway's own extraordinary and constant gilding and distortion of the truth – perhaps the symptom of a wish-fulfilment mechanism. *A Moveable Feast* turns out to be riddled with such untruths; and the other myths Hemingway set up come tumbling down too.

The great athlete won only one sporting event in his life – the flat distance dive at Oak Park High School. He was a clumsy boxer, and his stories of having fought professionally or as a sparring partner are 'unsupported by evidence'. In a friendly match in Paris with Canadian writer Morley Callaghan, with Fitzgerald acting as time-keeper, Hemingway was laid out; then he viciously blamed Fitzgerald for letting the round run on too long. The brave soldier of the First World War, who was reputed to have fought with an elite Italian corps of shock troops, had in fact never been in combat: he served with the Red Cross, was wounded by a mortar while distributing candy and cigarettes in 1918, and was hit by machine-gun fire while carrying a wounded man. His account of his poverty and dedication as a young writer in Paris may be seen in another light when we contemplate the fact that his wife Hadley was an heiress, and that his years of hunger included trips to Spain for the bullfights and skiing in the Austrian Alps.

But of all Hemingway's little liberties with the truth, the one that sticks longest in the throat is the famous reference to Fitzgerald in *The Snows of Kilimanjaro* – where, in the earlier editions, before he was asked to change it, he actually used Fitzgerald's name.

He remembered poor Scott Fitzgerald and his romantic awe of them [the rich] and how he had started a story once about them that began 'The very rich are different from you and me.' And how someone had said to Scott, 'Yes, they have more money.' But that was not humorous to Scott. He thought they were a special glamorous race and when he found that they weren't it wrecked him . . .

That 'poor Scott', used of a fine writer and friend who had given Hemingway nothing but devotion, is disgusting enough; but the story turns out to be not only untrue, but one in which Hemingway himself occupies the role in which he seeks to place Fitzgerald. In 1936 the editor Max Perkins and Hemingway had lunch with the critic Mary Colum, and Hemingway announced: 'I'm getting to know the rich.' To which Mary Colum replied: 'The only difference between the rich and other people is that the rich have more money.'

This misuse of his name was one of the very few things over which Fitzgerald remonstrated with Hemingway, and he did so with dignity. But to the very end, although they no longer saw each other, he was writing letters of appreciation concerning every book Hemingway published. Hemingway, meanwhile, surrounded by his cronies on fishing trips, would apparently hear no praise of Fitzgerald: when Arnold Gingrich tried it, he was shushed by yes-men.

When Ernest Hemingway died by his own hand, he was in deep depression and had written little of value for a long time. Scott Fitzgerald, when he died, regarded by the world as a failure, was fighting his drink problem successfully, and was doggedly in the middle of *The Last Tycoon*, whose quality clearly confirms that his genius was intact. Who was the failure, who the hero? A writer is not an athlete, not a civic leader, not a politician; his personality may be flawed and his life a ruin, but the one fight that defines him is the fight to stay with his work, and not to betray it. On those terms, 'poor Scott' was battling in the arena to the end, and his pathos is not the pathos of failure, but the pathos of greatness; and that greatness grows now year by year.

Back in 1927, writing to Hemingway, he had quotcd a line from *Men Without Women*, and had made a comment from the heart:

'In the Fall the war was always there but we did not go to it anymore.' God, what a beautiful line.

This says everything about Fitzgerald. How many writers so love the craft that they will single out one line of prose by a fellow writer and cherish it like that?

# Return to Hobart Town

The first sight of the island from the plane causes a leap of the heart, like the sudden appearance of a loved face. All returning Tasmanians experience this. Tugging at its moorings under the giant clouds of the Roaring Forties, Tasmania is different: we are no longer in Australia. All colours have the glassy intensity of a cold climate: the greens greener, the dark blue of the numberless hills and mountains appearing almost black, from the air.

Walking through Hobart at noon, I find that Mount Wellington has snow on its peak, in defiance of summer. The lunchtime crowds in the Elizabeth Street Mall have faces rosy with cold; the red brick paving, puddled from recent rain, is Dutch in its cleanliness; a busker sings 'Streets of London'. A pair of strolling police officers, male and female, in identical rainproof jackets, have the faces of twelve-year-olds: they look quite incapable of arresting anyone.

The mountain is a constant presence here, guarding the southwest wilderness, looming at Hobart's back. At the city's feet, visible from the mall, is one of the world's best deepwater harbours; but the port is dead. The masts and funnels which crowded it in my childhood, filling me with wild dreams of the world, have gone. The apple boats no longer load for London; the elegant tourists are no longer delivered from their giant overseas liners to Hadley's P & O Hotel. The estuary of the Derwent is vacant and bereft, staring towards Antarctica.

But the town itself is growing. The population has doubled

since my youth, and new suburbs are spreading through once-pastoral valleys. A few of the witless, multi-storey buildings no community can now escape have deformed the scale of a once perfectly proportioned colonial city; and in the last decade or so, Hobart has ceased to be provincial.

This happened with the coming of the gambling casino at Wrest Point, which was followed by an attendant swarm of restaurants, coffee shops and bistros. Many of the restaurants have higher standards than their equivalents in Sydney, and you can now eat *boeuf bourguignon* and Tasmanian crayfish in tastefully restored Georgian houses, in front of log fires, served by waiters and waitresses who have time to be friendly. It makes nightlife in Hobart a vast improvement on the 1950s, when our best choice lay between Anglo-Saxon hotel dining rooms smelling of old gravy, and the cabaret at Wrest Point for the Sandy Bay rich. But moving along Elizabeth Street, I muse inevitably on what's lost.

The second oldest city in Australia was still in many ways a village, thirty years ago, and the town's patterns were inside us, unnoted yet constant as the movement of the blood. Certain passers-by (never spoken to, their names never known) were inescapable as one's family. And I find myself still watching out for them. Where is the legless banjo-player in his wheelchair outside the Ship Hotel? Where are the two identical spinsters in their 1920s' cloche hats? And where is Reggie Wrong?

Our prominent senator and barrister Reggie Wright was well known to the Mainland; but only Hobart knew his counterpart, the other Reggie. Like all villages, we had our favourite fool, and Reggie's nickname was bestowed with cruel affection. Once, at this time of day, he would have been hurrying importantly along Elizabeth Street in his football club blazer, felt hat low over his eyes, arms held out from his plump body like the wings of a stumpy fowl, middle-aged face eager as a boy's. He would strut through Woolworth's and crow like a rooster at the girls behind the counters. They smiled on Reggie with queenly calm in their elegant black frocks, knowing as we all did that a small operation had once been performed on him by the authorities, to make him safe with girls. Or at least, we thought we knew this; perhaps it was a legend.

Many of the old shops have gone, which were here since first settlement. I hear them named in my head by my long-dead grandmother and vanished aunts, their slow voices certain of an unchanging world. 'I'll just go down to Mather's.' 'We'll pop along to Beck's.' In Beck's wonderful grocery store, with its adult pungencies of cheese and coffee, my mother and my grandmother would join a row of other matrons on spindly chairs at the counter, formal in hats, suits and gloves, while a whole platoon of brisk, smiling men in white aprons obeyed their every whim – running up tall ladders to high shelves; checking lists.

At home in our suburb of Newtown, my mother was served by an army of such tradesmen, without having to leave her door: the baker with his basket of bread; the milkman with his rattling cans. And in the winter, the strange figure of the Rabbit Man loomed out of the fog on his horse-drawn cart, with skinned little corpses all strung on wires – crying 'Rabby-o!' and ringing his brass bell. Stern-faced as a messenger from the underworld, in his big hat, he was more than a Rabbit Man to me.

The green trams are gone too, and I mourn them. Double-deckers brought us home from the beach, bucking along like horses. In the open top deck, legs tingling with sunburn, faces cooled by the wind, boys flicked wet towels at each other; and once a splendid madman leaped from the top deck on to the roof of a car below – for reasons that were never explained. The clanging of the trams was like the actual vibration of the town's nerves, and their rails had the significance of journey: silver lines to eternity. Out on the edge of the country, the waiting hum of a tram at its terminus was like the stitch and sound of Time. Grass grew around the foot of the timetable notice-board, and if you stirred a pebble, the noise was loud.

Here is Franklin Square, the town's nineteenth-century heart, its big old plane trees out in leaf. I look up at Sir John Franklin and inwardly salute him, as I always do. Chart in hand, the doomed explorer stands on his plinth in the middle of the ornamental pool, a sea gull perched as usual on his bald head, which wears a snowy cap of seagulls' droppings. Other gulls wheel and cry about him like the souls of his sailors, lost in the ice of the North-West Passage. We are fond of Franklin, in Tasmania: he was kindly, and one of our good governors; the information has been transmitted down the generations.

When Franklin and Lady Jane made their overland ex-pedition to the wild West Coast, they were brought back to Hobart on the schooner *Eliza*, under the command of my maternal great-great-grandfather, Captain James Hurburgh, who settled in Van Diemen's Land in 1837. The past is like a trunk in the attic here, very close at hand; ancestors are not far away. Above me, in the square, hover the spirits of two sailors; the famous rear admiral who is still hauntingly lost, preserved in the Arctic ice even now; and a humble merchant captain from Greenwich, who elected to stay on the southernmost edge of the world, and so sealed my fate.

One can walk all over Hobart in a few hours: this town of grandfathers. I am moving today through two earlier Hobarts, their ghostly after-images appearing all the time: the Hobart of the 1940s and my childhood, and the Hobart of the 1840s, and Captain Hurburgh: a sailors' town; a convict town. I wander through the well-preserved nineteenth-century suburb of Battery Point, perched on its ridge above the docks. It used to be 'bad', in my Depression infancy: a district of grim old poverty, its cottages built for dwarfs. Now it's an expensive historical filmset, full of tasteful paint and coach lamps: a real-estate man's dream. Here are the stone steps built especially for that Homeric whaling master, Captain James Kelly, whose trousers, in response to a bet, were proved to hold five bushels of wheat. Kelly's Steps take me down from the ridge on to Salamanca Place as they once took him; and here is Hobart of the 1840s.

The line of starkly simple freestone buildings along this wharf, erected by convicts, remains the finest colonial group in any Australian port. The buildings went through few transformations until recently; but today, colonial chic is in full bloom. Tamed into preciosity, loved to death, they house craft galleries, coffee bars and night spots for tourists with names like 'Mr Wooby's; and on weekends, open-air markets are set up in front of them.

One shouldn't complain, it's all very pleasant; but it's merely theatre, set against the backdrop of an extinct port; and these were once the ship's chandlers and brawling, roaring taverns of the whaling era, when Hobart was 'the New Bedford of the Southern Seas'. Fortunes were made, and a forest of masts rose beyond the quays: American and European whalers crowded to compete with the Tasmanians. It's recorded that on Good Friday in 1847, thirty-seven foreign whalers (many of them Americans) were refitting at Hobart Town. There was a fast link with San Francisco: ships heading for the gold rush revictualled here, and Hobart merchants supplied the American Pacific coast. The great whale-oil barrels were stacked where middle-aged hippies now ply their wares; sailors flush with money, back from the long trips, drank and fought and found their whores on Salamanca Place. Even twenty years ago, these buildings were still pubs, warehouses, sailmakers and small factories, whose doorways gave out essential odours of rope, bran, beer and jam.

In the 1950s, my mates and I drank in the last true sailors' pub here: the now-legendary Esplanade, known as the 'Blue House', whose proprietor was the even more legendary Elizabeth ('Ma') Dwyer. Its name meant exactly what it said: if you went in, you had to have a blue: a fight. Most of the clientele were merchant seamen; there were also a few petty criminals and shopworn ladies of the town. Ma's was known from Melbourne to London; but today it's just another example of colonial chic, with a twee sign outside the ground-floor bistro saying 'Ma's Bar'. None of its present clientele would have ventured inside the old pub.

My friends and I survived in there through cunning, rather than bravery. We bought drinks for the toughest-looking seamen in the bar on our first visit, and when a fight was offered to us by someone else, and a terrible fist thrust under our noses, our friend held up a warning hand. 'The boys are with me.' We had survived – for a time. Behind the bar, Ma Dwyer presided over the majestic din with absolute authority. Built like a small keg, with dyed orange hair and an expressionless white face by Toulouse-Lautrec, she rarely smiled; but when a Port Line boat was in, she would shout the bar, in memory of her late husband.

She tolerated fighting in the bar within limits; but when it threatened the rudimentary fittings (bare floor; wooden benches) she was capable of throwing the largest sailor out onto the esplanade: and he would let himself be thrown. Ma's rule was unquestioned. One night, two seamen were engaged in combat up and down the stairs outside, and Ma strode out and raised her powerful voice in warning. 'I don't mind youse fighting – but *stop bleeding on me stairs*!'

It's pleasant having a cappuccino or a wine in one of Hobart's charming new bistros, and I don't miss the milk bars or basic Greek cafés of the past. But I do miss Ma's.

# The Lost Hemisphere

Where does an Australian writer belong? Is he or she actually the product of a distinct culture? Is ours, in other words, a society that's different in any real way from the European source?

There was a time when I'd have bluntly answered no to that last question. Now, in the 1980s, I'm inclined to answer yes; and I'd like to explore the process that has caused me to change my mind. It may be that this process is really a sort of graph of what's been happening to Australia in the thirty-odd years since I began publishing my work.

When I answered no, I would have followed up by saying that those who pretended we belonged to a new and unique culture were just playing games. Moreover, as an Australian whose pioneer ancestors arrived in Tasmania and South Australia in the 1830s and 1840s, I would have felt entitled to my offensive opinion. These days, however, I would agree that we are beginning to see the emergence of a society whose differences from the source are real, and not a charade played by cosseted children. But first, let me dwell on the case for 'no'. It's a case with profound reasons where Australians of my generation are concerned. And it may well be that in the case of Tasmania, these reasons have a greater vividness than in most other parts of Australia.

My home was an island state that prided itself on being a

'second England'.* Feeling for what it called 'the mother country' has only recently withered away there: it's been a long dream, and it still lingers. Tasmania, more than most other parts of Australia, has been able to perform this role of 'another England' very successfully, simply because it has the right geography for it. I respect the power of geography in forming civilisations as Marxists respect economic determinism, and Tasmania's geographical situation has always seemed to me to be very strange and piquant. We who lived there between the thirties and the fifties were living in the half-light of a dying British Empire; but we only slowly came to realise it. The culture based on London was the imaginary pole star of our world; and there didn't seem a great incongruity in this. Consider the facts that make the island different. The entire land-mass of Australia – most of it flat and very dry – lies north of latitude forty. Tasmania, filled with mountains and hills, and containing more lakes than any comparable region except Finland, lies south of latitude forty, directly in the path of the Roaring Forties. It genuinely belongs to a different region from the continent: in the upside-down frame of the Antipodes, it duplicates northwestern Europe, while the continent is Mediterranean and then African. So it was very easy, in what was once Van Diemen's Land, for our great-grandfathers to put together the lost totality of England.

It began, of course, as a seabound jail, where the pickpockets from the rookeries of St Giles and Camden Town were dumped; but it was also another Kent, another Dorset, another Cumberland, for the free settlers. At the same time, it was on

---

* In the nineteenth century, when Anglo-Indians came there to recuperate from the heat, it was also known as the 'Sanatorium of India'.

the extreme southern rim of the world; one of the remotest places on earth. And it's always fascinated me to picture this perfect recreation of the lost home going on at the edges of Antarctic nothingness. Very soon the stage sets and the giant mirrors were complete: among gentle hills and green pastures that made it all perfectly natural, the great-grandfathers (my own among them) had freestone cottages with mullioned windows; hop fields and orchards; hawthorn hedges; climbing roses around outdoor privies; brutal boarding schools; Cockney sparrows to perch on slate roofs; rabbits to eat the crops; churches, brothels, and a thieves' kitchen by the Hobart docks called Wapping Old Stairs. In the midlands, the gentry mulled their claret in winter and rode to hounds.

In my childhood, the duplication remained complete. Our seasons were the seasons of my English story books. Snow fell in our midwinters, which were the winters of *Boy's Own Paper* and *The House at Pooh Corner*. I walked to school through London fogs. On the day that World War II broke out, the old English ladies who taught us at Clemes College were in tears. They explained to Grade Two the danger England was in, and my father's godmother thundered out 'There'll Always be an England' on the piano. We played German bombers in the playground, until we were made to play English bombers. Only Nobby Clark (now the Director of the National Institute of Dramatic Art) showed the misguided force of character to remain a German bomber, until he was shot down in flames. I had joined the English bombers with cowardly haste, desperately hoping to cover up my German name. I would fail.

The society that had produced us, so far away from what it saw as the centre of civilisation, made us rather like the prisoners in Plato's cave. To guess what the centre was like, that centre 12,000 miles away for which we yearned, we must study shadows on the wall, as our parents and grandparents had done. In each generation, these shadows had been found in books, magazines, the Saturday night cinema, the local repertory theatre. Noel Coward's *Bitter Sweet*, at the Hobart Repertory; the novels of Dickens, Louis Bromfield, Somerset Maugham, A. J. Cronin, Graham Greene: all shadows, clues to the real world we would some day discover in the northern hemisphere. America also appeared to us in the Saturday night films; but that was a different set of shadows. They weren't ours. Bill Sykes and the Napoleonic wars were as real in our minds as our ancestors were; as the dreaded and shameful memories of the convict stations at Port Arthur and Hell's Gates were.

But one felt the odd twinge of doubt. Who *were* we, marooned at 42 degrees south? Why were we *here*, and not *there*? And how perfect was the duplication really?

It was only on the surface, of course. The island's landscapes had a troubling strangeness, if you looked behind the stage sets we had erected. And beyond Port Davey's last little lights of settlement, in the extreme southwest, all normality ended. Beyond Port Davey there was nothing – there was Antarctica. In the Gothic wilderness of the southwest, 5000 square miles of impenetrable, cool-temperate rainforest lay entirely unsettled: a place where men had walked in and never walked out, and where rivers ran underground. A writer who is a native of such an island comes quite soon to the problem of trying to match its spirit with the spirit of the ancestral land in his head – the lost northern hemisphere. It's possible to love both, but matching them up isn't easy: the task of a lifetime, in fact.

What I am asserting is that this situation, to a great or lesser degree, is typical of many Australian writers, and that it's this tension – produced by the consciousness of another lost landscape and society – that produces a quality in Australian literature that is peculiar to it. It also produces a pathos of absence; so that the essential Australian experience emerges as one where a European consciousness, with European ancestral memories, is confronted by the mask of a strange land, and by a society still not certain of its style. I would find it difficult to argue with an Aboriginal who said that only his consciousness was truly in harmony with the land.

I know that this theme has been laboured often enough. It may also be considered outdated: something that only remains the concern of a past generation. I don't think so. It's one thing to decide, through an act of will, that you will cast off the grandfathers; cast off Europe. It's quite another successfully to do so in your soul. Everything has its pace and its season, and won't be hurried; and although the threads have now begun to snap, there's an almost unconscious level at which we're still a colony – and I mean this in the spiritual, not the political sense. Nations that have been colonies remain so for a long time, in spirit; and this has little to do with subservience. It has to do with history – one's own history – and it can no more be denied than our childhood. It's ours, for better or worse.

Here's an example of what I mean. Les Murray is one our most nationally conscious poets, as well as being one of our best. He is deeply rooted in the country of northern New South Wales in which generations of his family have farmed, and he is carrying out a one-man mission to tell Australians that they form a distinct culture which need go cap in hand to no one. I agree with him; but how far we can go – or should go – in cutting the deeper European roots is another matter. And Les

Murray himself, in many of his own poems, gives the game away.

> As we were rowing to the lakes
> our oars were blunt and steady wings
>
> the tanbark-coloured water was
> a gruel of pollen: more coming down
> hinted strange futures to our cells
>
> the far hills ancient under it
> the corn flats black-green under heat
> were cut in an antique grainy gold
>
> it was the light of Boeotian art.

Boeotia? Here is our most consciously Australian poet, in a passage of description of the New South Wales landscape which has vivid ease and precision, reaching for a classical association, and revealing as he does so a profoundly European consciousness. I point this out with no condescension; the situation is exactly how it should be, in my view. It would be just as foolish for us to discard our European inheritance as it would be (say) for an Indonesian to discard the Koran, or the Hindu myths.

This subjective situation of the Australian is simply so: and I can't see any problem in it. He is no longer a little duplicate Englishman – he hasn't been that for a long time; it was almost over by Henry Lawson's day. And he is now (if he is not Chinese, or an immigrant from South-East Asia) a European of mixed origins, dealing with a new hemisphere he has made his home (and in which he *is* at home), but which he has still to absorb fully into his unconscious. This continuing drama, and the drama of creating a new society here – a variant of the European model – is what much of Australian literature is about. In the novel, it's a constant thread, running through the work of such writers as Christina Stead, Patrick White and Randolph Stow.

The climate and landscape, too, in the hotter parts of Australia, are producing a spirit weirdly at odds with the original British one grafted on here. When I'm in Sydney, for instance, I often think of the essay Albert Camus wrote called 'Summer in Algiers'. Sydney in its hedonistic aspects, and the colonial Algiers Camus writes of, seem perfectly interchangeable.

This country has no lessons to teach . . . It is completely accessible to the eyes, and you know it the moment you enjoy it. Its pleasures are without remedy and its joys without hope . . .

During their entire youth men find here a life in proportion to their beauty. Then, later on, the downhill slope, and obscurity. They wagered on the flesh, but knowing they were to lose. In Algiers whoever is young and alive finds sanctuary and occasion for triumphs everywhere: in the bay, the sun, the red and white games . . . the cool-legged girls. But for whoever has lost his youth there is nothing to cling to and nowhere where melancholy can escape itself. Elsewhere, Italian terraces, European cloisters, or the profile of the Provençal hills – all places where man can flee his humanity and gently liberate himself from himself. But everything here calls for solitude and the blood of young men . . .

Between this sky and these faces turned towards it, nothing on which to hang a mythology, a literature, an ethic or a religion, but stones, flesh, stars and those truths the hand can touch.

The Sydney poet Geoffrey Lehmann seems to me to have expressed this spirit better than any other contemporary writer. In the cycles Lehmann has set in ancient Rome – *A Voyage of Lions* and *Nero's Poems* – he is really, I think, creating a double image: Rome and a transfigured Sydney for which Rome is a metaphor – a city of heat and water.

> While children fret and bang
> the table with a spoon,
> And wives strain to hear footsteps,
> and lonely migrants pace
> beneath our Roman moon
> Your concrete channel brings
>
> coolness to sultry courtyards,
> flowers and bean leaves lift
> beneath a tilting bucket . . .
>
> We rise from our siesta,
> file through the streets, each with
> a towel and a flask of oil,
> to bathe our innocent fat,
>
> the cripple in his litter,
> lovers who come late,
> this naked congregation
> of bodies washing off
> their dirt who celebrate
> a common love of water.

The voice is that of Nero Claudius Caesar, whose impish and demonic persona Lehmann puts on for this entire sequence. The Rome evoked is accurately and lovingly built up

from exact details; yet the musings quoted above could as well
be about marine Sydney, with its breathless inner-city nights
and its cheerfully hedonistic citizens: subjects of the big, brassy
sun. Lehmann's Rome-cum-Sydney, like Camus' Algiers, is
governed by pleasures taken cynically and without agonising.

> There's sand inside our bed.
> Jump up, shake out the sheet –
> We swam then slept, my hand
> prone on your lazy bottom –
> Now with each downward beat
> You flick sand at the sun.
>
> Our Golden Age is now.
> As sea-lights undulate
> and flicker on the walls,
> we lie without desire.
> Our bodies radiate
> the hours of sun we've shared.

Underneath this, there is the accompaniment of that faint,
paradoxical melancholy which is the penalty of worship of the
senses. In a poem called 'Night Flower', it imbues a youthful
night-scene from Sydney in the sixties, presented direct,
without its Roman mask.

> Sussex Street sleeps in mists of nickel moonlight
> And echoes ghostly music, but the sound
> Inside is crushing, voices, drums, stars jerked
> From electric guitars . . .
> Stung smiles, dark corridors where bodies push
> To a white stately room of bare feet stamping
> A gritty floor, figures dissolving in shadows,

> The dance, this great, sad, bitter swaying thing
> Which burns and moves and kisses us with salt.

Australians (rightly or wrongly) are now said to be among the least spiritually inclined, most pagan of all Western peoples; the physical gratifications so easily to be had in this country seeming to provide all that can be required of life. Perhaps Lehmann's Nero is speaking to them as well, when he defiantly reassures his antique subjects:

> I'll pass a law:
> 'Death is fact
> and after death there is nothing,
> and nothing is nothing to fear.'

The double strand of the European past and the Australian present is constant in Lehmann's work, as it is in that of a number of other poets and novelists where the sense of absence I've referred to recurs: a ghostly negative image of another landscape. And there is sometimes a mystical aspect to this: the apprehension of the 'other meaning' in landscape which is a central theme for the Tasmanian poet Vivian Smith.

> There is another meaning here – in birds
> and trees, in love and grief,
> in the fall of the blown leaf
> and pain and joy shuffled and dealt like cards
> – where thoughts in my stubborn land of pain
> travel like water over stone.

It remains to be said that there is also a mystery and presence in the body of the Australian land which is only itself, and which cannot be interpreted through the use of obverse images or hieroglyphs from the other hemisphere. Through an animistic device, Vivian Smith has given haunting expression to this land-spirit in a poem about the thylacine, or Tasmanian tiger – an animal supposedly extinct since the 1930s, but still fleetingly sighted from time to time in remote bush areas. Occasional searches have been mounted for it; so far in vain.

> They'll not find him in the hills:
> he's gone to earth in an unknown valley
> with legends of coal and Time in stone,
> with the sly fern, with the gully.

And Les Murray, in a poem set in the tall timber country of coastal New South Wales, crystallises the strange spirit of the bush through a paradox: the revelation that as with so much else in relation to the other hemisphere, things here are upside-down: opposite.

In here is like a great yacht harbour, charmed to leaves,
innumerable tackle, poles wrapped in spattered sail,
or an unknown army in reserve for centuries.

Flooded-gums on creek-ground, each tall because of each.
Now a blackbutt in bloom is showering with bees
but warm blood sleeps in the middle of the day.
The witching hour is noon in the gum forest.

2

The case for 'yes', like the case for 'no', hinges on that intimate evolution I've just been discussing: a coming-to-terms with strangeness in the soul. Like ageing, or learning slowly to love someone, such a process doesn't seem particularly marked while it's happening, nor even inevitable; then, one day, we find it's final. Meanwhile, on another, external and pragmatic level, a set of developments has been going on in Australia which has to do with our vitality as an independent national community, and our altered relationship with Britain and Europe. At this level, the changes since my youth in the 1950s have been very great indeed.

When I went to London at twenty-two, English publication and English critical approval were still the twin pinnacles for which an Australian novelist strove. But today the situation has partly reversed itself. The really significant critical reception now is the one we get at home. England, drifting farther away from us, is more and more inturned, no longer as interested as she was in her crude children. And the vitality of the creative scene in Australia generally is such that this doesn't matter as much as it once did. One must qualify this by saying that a novelist always wants as big a market as possible for his work, and that both English and American publication remain very desirable, if only because of the small size of the Australian market. But what has changed is the fact that the response to a novel out here is what will do most to give it continuing life; and it will usually be best understood by Australian readers and critics. We are no longer a British province; we are a foreign country, and there are nuances and family jokes in our writing (and in our films and our painting) that only the native can fully understand; small shocks of recognition that cannot quite be shared. Paradoxically, just at the point where our films and our fiction in particular are arousing new interest internationally, it is the audience at home we think of first. We worry about the other audiences later.

This of course has very important implications for any

creative artist. A writer can't finally escape his own country; what your own people think of what you have made for them – that's what hurts if they put thumbs down; that's what gives greatest joy if they put thumbs up. But more importantly, I don't believe it's possible for a writer to portray at any great depth a people other than his own. I can't easily get under the skins of any other people than Australians, however much I travel, simply because I don't fully *know* any other people. I could portray an Englishman or a Frenchman from the outside, but only with difficulty from the inside. And this hinges on the importance of childhood. You can't know a people unless you know what their childhood was; and if we cut the thread that links us to that country, we lose our bearings.

This is not as limiting as it might seem, particularly since Australia's identity, in this post-colonial period, is rapidly changing. Geography being the great shaper of human development that it is, New Guinea and our nearest South-East Asian neighbours – in particular Indonesia – are assuming an inescapable importance in Australia's future. Young Australians make the pilgrimage to Asia as often now as they make the pilgrimage to Europe – and inevitably, as young writers undergo formative experiences in Asia, they will set their work there. We will then have to become less narrow in deciding what constitutes a work of 'Australian literature'. There are still those who hold the curious view that it must be set within our boundaries in order to qualify.

I was once asked by a visiting Japanese professor of literature: Why do you not set more books in Tasmania? Why did you set *The Year of Living Dangerously* in Indonesia? We need more books set in Tasmania, he said. This was flattering – but limiting, I thought. Literature isn't sociology, it isn't about filling needs for social observation, and one simply can't predict where the lightning of imagination will strike next. An Australian has as much right to set his books in Jakarta, Hong Kong or Bangkok and still be regarded as an Australian writer, as an English novelist has to set *his* work there – or in Paris – and still be regarded as part of the English literary scene. The Asian–Pacific region in particular is our territory, and our writers may well do a lot to define it: even perhaps to give it configurations it didn't have before, which literature has a habit of doing.

In the long view of history, our umbilical cord to Britain was cut only yesterday, and we have hardly taken more than a few timid steps, imaginatively, into the Asian–Pacific world. And I think this is natural. There is a glib habit of saying we are 'part of Asia', and that we'd better get on with it. It's not going to be so quick and easy – and this glibness may be why we've done far too little to build real connections with the fascinating world just beyond our boundaries, although we trek through it on our tourist holidays. It's a glibness which tries to throw out the European inheritance which is our greatest cultural treasure, and which also treats with foolish complacency the diverse and rich Asian cultures we seek to make connection with. The one cannot lightly be discarded; the other cannot instantly be put on. And the cliché is geographically inaccurate. We are not 'part of Asia': Australia is a South Pacific nation, and through sheer weight and its degree of progress, one of the most important. Indonesia is not 'part' of our immediate location; it's with the South Pacific nation of New Guinea that we have our closest physical links. But Indonesia, where Asia begins, is our most considerable neighbour, and must therefore be a part of our political and cultural destiny. And because it's where Asia begins, it must fascinate us.

'Only connect,' to use E. M. Forster's words. How are we to connect with Indonesia, with Malaysia, with Singapore? Real connection will not come through the sterile chatter of conferences and cultural missions. It will come when individual Australians, Indonesians, Malaysians and Singaporians begin to visit each other, and to examine and portray each other's different worlds. It will come when we work at common projects. It will come when we recognise the fact that we have different cultural identities, accept the differences, and look for the points of contact. In small ways, it's already happening; and we are moving inch by inch towards more significant fusions. I can't imagine what these fusions will be like, but I know they will happen.

Meanwhile, this is the calm before the storm, for Australia. There is an old Chinese curse which runs: 'May you live in interesting times.' Australia is about to live in interesting times. When the British quit Singapore, that was a turning-point for us as fateful as the withdrawal of the Roman legions from Britain. When we have fully understood this, a new South Pacific nation will have been born. Yes, it will be a hybrid; but it may be a hybrid of some vitality. How that vitality is used will be another story.

# A Tasmanian Tone

A long time ago, I was crossing to Maria Island, off Tasmania's east coast, in a small boat. The group I was with included the poet Vivian Smith. It was the first time he and I had been across there, and both of us found the seascape around us strange and unfamiliar, although both of us were native Tasmanians. The grey-green swell; the cold, stark light; the mournful, deserted island with its ruined convict station: what did they remind us of?

We imagined the scene to be like the Hebrides – although neither of us had been to Scotland. But we finally concluded that it probably resembled nowhere else: it was simply itself, and Tasmanian. We were victims, we realised, of a colonial habit of mind – always seeking other landscapes in our own. And Vivian said something then that I've often remembered: that a country and its landscapes perhaps don't fully exist until they've been written about – until poets and novelists create them.

What neither of us realised at the time was that this idea had already been thought about in Tasmania just over a hundred years earlier, and set down on paper. In 1851, an Irish political prisoner, transported to newly settled Van Diemen's Land because of his writings denouncing the British government of his country, found himself at Lake Sorell in the central highlands. Enchanted by the place, he wrote:

> As we float here at our ease we are willing to believe that no lake on earth is more beauteous than Sorell. Not so

berhymed as Windermere is this Antarctic lake . . . not so famous in story as Como or Geneva . . . Why should not Lake Sorell also be famous? Some sweet singer shall berhyme thee yet. Every bay will have its romance, and the glancing of thy sun-lit, moon-beloved ripples shall flash through the dreams of poets yet unborn.

The writer was John Mitchel, whose *Jail Journal* is one of the best things in colonial Australian literature. Mitchel was a most unusual convict: a Protestant gentleman and publisher, whose campaign against British rule in Ireland had made him celebrated in Europe. Youthful, handsome, and one of the most eloquent of the Irish activists, his adventures and imprisonment reported in the Paris press, Mitchel was a great embarrassment to the British, who never at any stage imprisoned him, and who allowed him to bring out his family and his library and to buy land. He was thus given considerable freedom and comfort in Tasmania, provided he did not try to escape the island. This he finally did, however, making a successful, swashbuckling flight to America in 1853, disguised as a priest.

With Mitchel's journal, Tasmanian writing of quality begins. The vivid (though admittedly flowery) descriptions of Van Diemen's Land in his journal are rarities to be treasured, since very few intellectuals of Mitchel's type came there at that time. Most of the descriptions we have of early Tasmania are by limited or prosaic men. But with Mitchel, we are looking at the early scenes and the first settlers of the island through the filter of a genuinely poetic imagination: pictures of a society on the edge of wilderness by an impassioned activist and man of action with the sensibilities of an artist.

Mitchel's thoughts, as the journal reveals, were bent from

the first on escape; he longed to get back to Europe, out of a society he considered barbaric, and a British prison. But he was won over in spite of himself by the beauty of the Tasmanian landscape, in which he saw mirages of Ireland everywhere.

> In vain I try to torment myself into a state of chronic, savage indignation: it will not do here. In vain I reflect . . . that these ancient mountains with the cloud-shadows flying over their far-stretching woodlands, are but Carthaginian prison walls – that the bright birds are but 'ticket of leave' birds, and enjoy only 'a comparative liberty'. In vain – there is in the soul of man a buoyancy that will not let it sink to utter despair.

Have Mitchel's predictions on Lake Sorell come true? Is there a Tasmanian literature? The question is merely fanciful, since only a few novelists and poets have yet written about Tasmania at all, and fewer still who were native-born. But what can be seen already, I think, is that there's a regional tone in writing set in Tasmania: a quality that the island stamps on it. Mitchel foresaw it, riding through the bush, inhaling the air of the highlands. And musing on the pristine peace of Lake Sorell, prophesying 'the dreams of poets yet unborn', he saw the 'jet black, proud-crested swan of the Antarctic forest waters' as a reverse image of the white swans of the northern hemisphere: an image just as beautiful.

Vivian Smith is probably most distinctly that native-born poet of Tasmania whom John Mitchel conjured up, publishing his first poems exactly a hundred years after the Irish rebel rode out to his unspoiled lake at the end of the world. Exploring every aspect of the Tasmanian landscape with lyric penetration, Smith has even written of the swans.

I came down to the tideless bay
from hills sketched in rain
to light that flickers the pencil reed
to where these swans remain

and sail with slim and supple necks
over the water's rippled weed,
with necks and shadows seeking
in the cautious lengthening shade . . .

And there, now here, these seven swans,
this water-world's remembered skies
hold silence, weed, and living shade
within my centre of surprise.

Kenneth Slessor, in his introduction to the poems which Vivian Smith and I contributed many years ago to *The Penguin Book of Modern Australian Verse*, speculated on the way that Australia's vast geographic differences might affect the work of its writers, producing regional characteristics. He wrote:

> It is not unlikely that the humidity of [Australia's] north, the dryness of the centre, the frigidity of the extreme south, are being increasingly reflected in the characters of the people.

And he spoke of the 'glacial background' in both Vivian Smith's verse and mine, and of a possible 'Tasmanian style' that was emerging, based on images and mannerisms. Nowhere is this better exemplified, I believe, than in one of Vivian Smith's poems whose subject is the island itself. It's a style which combines wistfulness, spareness and a glassy clearness: the tonality of the landscape itself, with its cool-temperate light and its stark, sharp-edged lines.

Water colour country. Here the hills
rot like rugs beneath enormous skies
and all day long the shadows of the clouds
stain the paddocks with their running dyes . . .

Beyond the beach the pine trees creak and moan,
in the long valley poplars in a row,
the hills breathing like a horse's flank
with grasses combed and clean of the last snow.

Vivian Smith has gone on to become a poet of universal themes,
his work set in other latitudes, both in Australia and abroad.
But there is a sense in which Slessor's perception has proved
true: the vision is a unique one, nurtured by our cool island in
the path of the Roaring Forties. The seas below its southern
coast are among the wildest in the world; fishing boats out of
Hobart can disappear there without trace, and one of Smith's
poems about lost relatives has a coloration and feeling that
could have come from nowhere else – except perhaps from that
northern hemisphere that Tasmania so irresistibly recalls.

Someone said dead men make islands in the sea
but there are no trees, no green islands
growing from these mouths and hollow eyes.
Under the areas of empty sea they lie,
fishermen drowned in a storm all miles from land . . .

There are no green islands for the coastless birds;
no trees branching from those eyes to hang a thought upon;
nothing, nothing that the hands can find:
only another island, quiet and simple, forming in another
    mind.

Island people are a little different from those belonging to a continent; their feeling for native place isn't necessarily more intense, but is perhaps more intimate. The island can be contained in the mind; it's yours, almost as your house is yours; to be away from it is always exile, and the theme of exile runs through Smith's later work, written in Sydney. But there's another theme in the Tasmanian mind, haunting its fiction in particular. This is the theme of the convict.

The convict past is like a wound, scarring the whole inner life of Tasmanians. It's taken lightly nowadays; but Tasmanians of my generation remember when the suspicion of convict ancestry was a matter of real shame and anguish – even up to the 1950s. That past was hated. In my boyhood, considerably less than a century had elapsed since the disbandment of the British penal settlement at Port Arthur on the Tasman Peninsula south of Hobart; and the site wasn't then the cheerful tourist attraction that it's become today. It was openly or secretly loathed. Despite the beauty of the blue bay, the bush-covered hills, the village-green-coloured grass and the honeyed sandstone of the ruined penitentiary, it wasn't a pleasant place to visit: oppressively silent, its very air seemed heavy with sullen sorrow, and the small licking of wavelets on the pebbles was somehow ominous. I had an ancestral connection with Port Arthur: Captain James Hurburgh, my great-great-grandfather, master of the schooner *Eliza*, had made a regular run here from Hobart Town; and one of the *Eliza*'s duties had been to chase runaway convicts 'who might carry off any colonial shipping'. I have not yet discovered a transported convict in my ancestry – which isn't to say one mightn't turn up – but despite the fragile respectability of my link with the settlement, the same resentful disquiet affects me when I go there as affects many other Tasmanians.

To comprehend the depth of this feeling, one has only to consider a little-known fact about the penal station's end. The stone buildings there today are mere, ruined shells; and I used to wonder why. Many people imagine this fate has come upon them through antiquity – anything over a hundred years being antiquity in Australia. But solid stone buildings with all their fittings don't get into that condition naturally in a mere hundred-odd years, and nor did these – even though fires and poor materials account for some of the damage. After transportation ended and the settlement was disbanded in 1877, the Hobart city fathers told the local building contractors to go into Port Arthur and take what they liked. The place was gutted; and it's difficult not to see this as a symbolic act of hatred by the free settlers, who had fought to end the shame of being a penal colony. Tasmania (its very name having been changed from the one with such grim associations wherever English was spoken) was trying to erase its past.

But of course, it would fail; the past refuses to be erased, no matter how much evidence is destroyed, and the only way left to remove the difficulty is through a collective amnesia. This too was attempted. Tasmanians when I was young didn't want to know anything about their antecedents beyond the two sets of grandparents; a deliberate vagueness and indifference being assumed about any more remote ancestry. And working as a temporary archivist in the State Archives many years ago, I learned of the lengths to which some respectable Hobart citizens would go to deal with the problem. A leading Hobart merchant, whose now-vanished stationery business was prominent in the town, had come in and asked to see if his great-grandfather was in the convict registers. The register was duly brought to him, since in those days they were open to the public; and he took the great volume away to a quiet table to study the entry for his ancestor, transported for stealing geese. When the archivists went to retrieve the register, both the respectable merchant and his ancestor's torn-out page had vanished.

A journalist friend of mine, on finding that I had access to these secret records, asked me to make the predictable investigation on his behalf. He was diverted and amused, being of a younger generation than the prominent merchant, when I turned up with an ancestor: a felon transported in 1842. But his father, on learning the news, was less delighted. He went deathly white, my friend told me, and said quietly: 'The aunts must never learn of this.'

I remember too the curious attitude people had in my childhood towards Marcus Clarke's celebrated novel, *For the Term of his Natural Life*. Many had read this nineteenth-century epic of the convict days in Tasmania, and most of them seemed to regard it with solemn respect. ('You look like Gabbett,' my mother would say, when I appeared in an unkempt state at the table. She was referring to the terrible convict turned cannibal who ate his mates, and whom Clarke had based on the actual case of Alexander Pierce.) But this respect in which the book was held was mixed with a sort of distaste, as though it contained lapses into pornography. It would have been better, the faces said, had it never been written. They didn't want to be reminded; and copies were not easy to come by. The father of one of my schoolmates, when we questioned him about it, was franker. 'It's a terrible book,' he burst out. 'Terrible. It shouldn't be read about any more, the things they did to those convicts. It should be banned.' I felt he was afraid of it; children have such insights.

Today, in a period when images of horror and suffering are taken for granted in our entertainments, Clarke's book has lost some of its forbidding power to shock; it has dwindled into a staid Victorian historical novel, well-researched and grimly realistic, with a Dickensian propensity for melodrama and coincidence. Yet its narrative strength, and the vividness of its recreation of the grim old penal colony, remain impressive; and even today it's difficult to read with indifference the episodes detailing the trials of the unlucky Rufus Dawes at Port Arthur and Macquarie Harbour. This latter was the most dreaded of all the penal stations. Port Arthur, by comparison, was a pleasant place; and indeed by the harsh standards of its day it was a model prison, run with scrupulous attention to detail. But Macquarie Harbour, known as Hell's Gates, was the isolated settlement on the wild west coast of Tasmania where 'incorrigibles' were sent; and it clearly rivalled in its cruelty any of this century's concentration camps. Convicts murdered each other so that hanging would free them from their sufferings (it was 'better than where they were', they said), and the only escape was into icy, unexplored rainforest lashed by the Roaring Forties: bush so impenetrable that starvation was almost certain there – unless, like Pierce, men took to cannibalism.

Clarke's novel makes this real in a way that objective history can never do; in a way that has lodged permanently in the Australian collective memory. Reading passages like the following, in which Dawes, according to standard practice, is forced by the sadistic Commandant Burgess to flog a fellow convict – a boy too feeble to take it, who subsequently dies – an old anger stirs, passed down through the blood. The passage is true in every detail to scores of well-documented cases.

> Kirkland had ceased to yell now, and merely moaned. His back was like a bloody sponge, while, in the interval between the lashes, the swollen flesh twitched like that of a new-killed bullock. Suddenly, Macklewain saw his head droop on his shoulder. 'Throw him off! Throw him off!' he cried, and Troke hurried to loosen the thongs.
>
> 'Fling some water over him!' said Burgess, 'he's shamming.'
>
> A bucket of water made Kirkland open his eyes. 'I thought so,' said Burgess. 'Tie him up again.'
>
> 'No. Not if you are Christians!' cried North.
>
> He met with an ally where he least expected one. Rufus Dawes flung down the dripping cat. 'I'll flog no more,' said he.

These ghosts still hover in the mind, in Tasmania; and perhaps in the landscape itself. In *Night Run*, a short story by James McQueen – another native Tasmanian – the memory surfaces in a moment which is both physical and psychic:

> The old familiar towns slid past; Campbell Town, Ross, Tunbridge . . . silent facades of worn sandstone and decaying brick, sweating the night-cold sweat of their builders, convicts a hundred years dead.

The late Hal Porter, who spent much time in Tasmania, took as his subject in *The Tilted Cross* the nineteenth-century Van Diemen's Land of convict and gentry, expending on it a brilliant and baroque wealth of detail suggesting Dickens crossed with Ronald Firbank. But Porter's final vision of the place is Gothic:

> Van Diemen's Land, an ugly trinket suspended at the world's discredited rump, was freezing. From horizon to horizon stretched a tarpaulin of congealed vapour so tense that it had now and then split, and had rattled down a vicious litter of sleet like minced glass, that year, that winter, that day.
>
> It was the privy of London ... turnkey-ridden and soldier-hounded. No one returned over the crags except bushrangers, crazed from suppers of human flesh, and chattering a litany learned in a hinterland of horror. There was nowhere to go in Hobart Town except Hobart Town.

Hal Porter was a Victorian, and saw mostly the exotic and grotesque in Tasmania. His is a foreigner's vision. I make this distinction between writers who are immigrants to the island and those who are native-born since nothing conditions a writer so much as the place in which he grew up. To the native-born, Tasmania is normality, and the sun-levelled continent to the north is alien; a physical love of the island's landscape is an ineradicable part of his nature. Certainly this is so of James McQueen, who displays in his prose both a Tasmanian identification with place and the same ability as Vivian Smith to depict exactly the hillbound landscape and its ice-clear southern weather:

> On one of these bright cold mornings they squatted beside their tiny fire, enamel mugs hot between their palms, a small chill breeze rippling the feathery tips of the wattles behind

them and swaying the tall silver-stippled trunks a little. Before them the meshing spurs of foothills, hills, low mountains stretched away for fifty miles. In the thin crystal air the rock faces of the mountains showed in clear etched detail, the snow on the peaks so white that the shadows seemed almost indigo. The trees of the distant forests were not hazed, but a delicate smoke-coloured filigree.

John Mitchel, like many other settlers in Tasmania, then and since, quickly noticed its climatic and physical similarities to the latitude from which he'd been exiled. 'Gardens,' he wrote, 'are a luxury to which this soil and climate afford all facilities and temptations. All the flowers that grow in English gardens ... thrive and flourish here with little care ... There is now hardly a settler's house without hedges of sweetbriar ... The genial kindness of this climate to all sorts of animal and vegetable life is admirable to behold ...' And he wrote of 'caves floored with silvery sand, shell-strewn, such as in European seas would have been consecrated of old to some Undine's love'.

This response to Tasmania continues to occur in those Australian writers and artists who emigrate to the island from other states. It can be seen in the work of the late James McAuley, who settled there in middle age, and in whose later poetry are both the spirit of the island he fell in love with and the lingering Europe he saw there, interwoven as harmoniously as a motif in a tapestry.

> A dark-green gum bursts out in crimson flowers.
> Old people slowly rot along the wall.
> The young ones hardly notice them at all.
> Both live in the same picture-book of hours.

Four-turreted a square tower balks the sky,
Casting a shadow; an organ softly plays.
The afternoon wears out in a gold daze.
On ragged wings, uttering its carking cry

A raven scavenges . . .

Geography is the great hidden shaper of history and character. The essence in landscape and climate will always impose itself on the human spirit, and especially the writer's spirit, more finally and insidiously than anything else, in the end; and this small, stormy island in the world's utmost south will continue to impose its own – even when the ghosts of the other landscape, that history in the head, have faded from gulleys and lanes and mountainsides; even if sweetbriar ceases to be grown around cottage doors. There's already a Tasmanian tone, for those who care to listen, which owes little to the past but much to the island itself, and to the silent croon within it. The tone springs from a sense of waiting in the landscape: the tense yet serene expectancy of some nameless revelation. Here it is most purely in the verse of Gwen Harwood:

Ocean, heaven, the same colour.
Bruny lies between
unruffled sky, unclouded water.
Colours of solitude surround us.
Shadows of gentle green
brush the planes of thigh and shoulder . . .

'How will you paint me this green air
and the distant fields' autumnal shimmer?'
– As you will sing a dream of leaves
through which the heavens fall like water.

# Mysteries

*Go out and camp somewhere. You're lying down.*
*A wind comes, and you hear this 'Mapooram'.*
*'What's that?' you say. Why that's a Mapooram.*
*You go and find that tree rubbing itself.*
*It makes all sorts of noises in the wind . . .*

*A Wirreengun, a clever-feller, sings*
*that tree. He hums a song, a Mapooram:*
*A song to bring things out, and close things*
*up . . .*

> *Mapooram*, related by
> the Aboriginal Fred Biggs to the poet
> Roland Robinson

There are many variants on the basic myth of the visit to Fairyland. In a version from the Austrian Tyrol, it runs like this.

A herdsman one day followed his cows across a hillside, and under a great stone, and so into a cave. There he was met by a lady. She gave him food, and led him into a strange, gentle countryside, where she offered him work as a gardener. He found the place so enchanting that he accepted her offer; and for a time he forgot his home, his family, and the life he had left outside. The air of that place was always balmy, its food delicious, its wine like nectar, and its people of unearthly beauty, since these were fairies.

But after a time the man grew homesick, and begged to be allowed to return to the outer world. He was allowed to do so; but when he got back, everything looked different – and no one recognised him except one old crone. She came up to him and said: 'Where have you been? I've been looking for you for two hundred years.' And she took him by the hand and he fell dead; for she was Death.

Fairy stories like this were rarely meant for children, but were messages of warning; and perhaps this one holds a warning for the present era. The West seems currently to long for a return to the time when myth was paramount, and magic real, and to be more and more preoccupied with illusion. We spend long hours with the shadows on our video machines; our stores are full of books on legends and fairy-lore for adults; our science fiction imitates ancient fables, and more and more of our films are recreations of myth and fable as well. And we seem, at least for a good proportion of our time, to be living at second-hand. We talk constantly of 'roles' and 'images' and 'fantasies'. We are all actors, it seems, on some insubstantial stage, whose identities and even genders may at any moment dissolve.

But there's a penalty for addiction to illusion, as the stories of the visit to Fairyland have always insisted; and the penalty is some sort of death. We wake on the hillside not only to discover a fatal loss of time, but that our fantasy has emptied us of the will to live; masturbation of the spirit has drained us of our capacity to love what's real. Addicted to Elfland's dream and perversity, we waste away.

The West is no longer – officially at any rate – a Christian society. Few people seem to be asking what sort of society it is, perhaps because it was tacitly agreed some time ago that its new basis would be scientific humanism. But has this really turned out to be true? As far as the counter-culture is concerned – and a good deal of our popular culture as well – it is plainly not so at all; instead, we have a society that's increasingly reaching back to paganism: to worship of the earth, and to the myths and beliefs and values of the pre-Christian world. In fact, we probably vie with the fourteenth century as one of the peak periods of fragmenting belief – with an accompanying absorption in witchcraft, magic, and the occult.

It's become commonplace to point this out, but less commonplace to discuss the possible consequences; and some of these are not so agreeable as others.

In 1975, at a coroner's inquest in Wakefield, Yorkshire, it was found that Michael Taylor had killed his wife by tearing out her eyes and tongue with his bare hands. He told police that he had to kill her 'to get rid of the evil' in her. Taylor had been involved with a Christian Fellowship group, and was emotionally attracted to Marie Robinson, a girl preacher who was friendly with both himself and his wife. Four days before the murder, he had menaced Miss Robinson, who told the inquest that he became transformed and 'bestial', that he screamed and babbled 'in tongues', and that she believed the Taylor home was a focus of demonic activity. On the night of the murder, Taylor had undergone an all-night rite of exorcism, together with five other people, which was performed by the Reverend Peter Vincent. But Mr Vincent said that he believed three evil spirits had not been expelled, and that if Taylor went home to his wife there could be serious trouble; 'even murder'. The finding of the coroner's court, and the pronouncements of a psychiatrist who examined Taylor, were somewhat extraordinary, and yet perfectly consistent with the philosophical and moral positions underlying both our present judicial system and our view of the human mind and spirit. It was decided that Christine Taylor's death was due to 'misadventure': that is, it had been caused neither by murder nor by accident. And Taylor was found not guilty of murder by reason of insanity, and sent to Broadmoor, the hospital for the criminally insane.

The examining psychiatrist there attributed Taylor's insanity, and the murder itself, to his activities with the Christian Fellowship group, and to the exorcism which had been performed on him. So far, so good. Atrocious acts of this kind, of a type once called 'evil', are generally explained by insanity, and we are satisfied. But although the psychiatrist found that shortly after the death of his wife Taylor was 'detached from reality', and considered him to be suffering from acute schizophrenia, he changed his opinion, while the hearing was still going on, as a result of a long interview with Taylor. The patient gave a lucid account of the events leading to his wife's death, and the psychiatrist stated that he was 'a stable, intelligent, hard-working young man with no sign of mental illness'. This, however, did not alter the doctor's opinion that he must have been temporarily insane on the night of the killing; nor did it alter the court's judgement. The idea of the action of supernatural evil was not to be considered by authorities representing a society whose laws and sciences are based on the premises of materialistic rationalism. Insanity had to be the only possible cause of these events, and therefore insanity was pronounced to be the cause. No charge of murder was made, and the psychiatrist's opinion on the matter was that Taylor had been inflicted with other people's views which 'had probably caused him a great deal of stress and disturbance'. Although Taylor was still hospitalised, he was declared legally and clinically sane. But, reported the psychiatrist, 'he has the stress of having to live with what he has done.' The Reverend Vincent, who was seen by the medical authorities as at least partly the cause of Taylor's troubles, said that the murder was the result of possession. The Archbishop of Canterbury said that in future, church exorcists should work with psychiatrists.

Since the seventies, reports in the press of incidents like this have become so frequent that they scarcely arouse surprise any more. Another type of story has also become frequent, typified by one from Apollo Bay in Victoria, Australia. The corpse of a naked woman was found in 1975 bearing marks that suggested ritual killing. One arm had been removed, and a one-armed voodoo doll was found with the body. This case is discussed by Neville Drury, an authority on the occult, in his book *Other Temples, Other Gods*; and in that book, Drury and co-author Gregory Tillett claim that there are several small groups in Australia employing a sort of Aboriginal voodoo. These groups are said to be composed of Aborigines and Europeans, and to employ a mixture of magical traditions:

> In one city they are said to meet on nights of the full moon, and to engage in semi-naked dancing round an open fire, whilst chanting and clapping rhythmically. Ritual sacrifice of chickens, and ceremonial use of blood ... have been reported. Another report, from an elderly woman, included details of ceremonies based on traditional aboriginal religion, but modified after the fashion of Western Satanism, involving the ritual sacrifice of chickens and dogs, and a variant on 'pointing the bone'.

Such reports of a return to paganism and the demonic, in an age which until quite recently regarded such things as relics of cultural infancy, jostle for attention in the media, and we get glimpses of strange depths beneath the bizarre cases of rape and murder. The most extraordinary in recent years (still unresolved at the time of writing) has been the Azaria Chamberlain affair. Lindy Chamberlain, the wife of a Seventh Day Adventist pastor, was found guilty of having murdered her infant daughter Azaria at a camping ground near Ayers Rock, in the Central Australian desert, in August 1980. The child's throat was alleged to have been cut, on the evidence of blood in the Chamberlain car, but the body has never been found. Michael Chamberlain was found to be an accomplice in the crime. On the night of her baby's death, Mrs Chamberlain set off an alarm, claiming that a dingo had made off with the infant, taking it from the family's tent. A search proved fruitless. The Chamberlains have launched appeals costing millions, and at present Lindy Chamberlain is free from jail, the subject of constant media attention, and of a number of books. What gives the case its peculiar and sensational overtones is the fact that the couple have been the subjects of persistent rumours linking them to the demonic as an explanation of the motive for the killing. It has been claimed that the child's name, Azaria, means in translation 'a sacrifice in the desert'. There are also stories that prior to her death, she was dressed in black baby clothes, and that the police found a small coffin in the Chamberlain house. True or not, these stories typify an era which is filled with antique and sinister echoes; and weird coincidences also surround the affair. Ayers Rock is known to the Aborigines as Uluru, the place of Kurpanngu, the 'devil dingo'; and one of the many caves in the rock is called Cut Throat . . .

The new era of mysticism and the irrational we have entered was hatched on the American West Coast in the mid-sixties.

Witches claim it began in 1966: the year of Satan's numbers. But certainly it began roughly about the time when Timothy Leary called on young Americans to 'tune in, turn on and drop out.' 'New Age consciousness' began then: a consciousness that is spreading yearly, giving birth to a multitude of cults and new religions. Drury and Tillett, in their book, claim that Australia is an important centre for 'New Age' occult movements; and they describe one based in Western Australia which presents a classic profile. This group is waiting for the present social, economic and political order to collapse. Its members will then survive a holocaust of fire by which the earth is to be purified, after which they will be liberated in flying saucers, ultimately returning to start a new civilisation. It thus embodies most of the features of this type of movement all over the Western world: movements which cluster most thickly in California, another desert region. Always announced by prophet or Messiah figures, the cults range through a spectrum which includes genuine mysticism, theories of a comic-book naivety, and at the ultimate extreme, the sort of group derangement which ends in the horror of Jonestown, with its mass suicide, its rows of bodies stinking in the sun.

There's an important and interesting meaning in the new paganism, and few writers have dealt with the spiritual revolution that's going on better than Colin Wilson. In book after book, Wilson has analysed the occult with an intellectual clarity and power to synthesise that's enjoyable and impressive; and this is accompanied by a stimulating optimism about human destiny that's currently rare. In one of these works, entitled *Mysteries*, he has made what he calls an attempt to write the *Principia* of psychic science. This may seem a strange place to find a message of hope for the future of man – but it does contain one. And Wilson submits his proposition only after assembling plenty of evidence, in the best scientific manner. Towards the end, he sums up:

> The human organism . . . is an enormous computer, containing thousands, probably millions, of circuits that we never use. Absurd and paradoxical as it sounds, man is actually a god. His capacities are superhuman. What seems to have gone wrong is that he has allowed himself to become subject to some kind of law of diminishing returns that has reduced him to a mere fraction of his stature.

This has been a thread running through Wilson's work ever since his first, youthful publication, *The Outsider*. Since that book, which concerned those poets and visionaries driven by a craving for both deeper knowledge and a sort of absolute freedom, Wilson has obsessively pursued what he calls 'the paradoxical nature of freedom' in all his writing. In *Mysteries*, he makes the final statement that 'consciousness *is* freedom' – and by this he means a new dimension of consciousness: a new stage of evolution.

Man's freedom, Wilson says, is not illusory; it's always possible. But a man relaxing in an armchair may be bound by invisible fetters of boredom, of spiritual poverty, because of the narrowness of his consciousness. Our task is to widen consciousness. Man's being, he says, is like a vast mansion; yet he seems to prefer to live in a single room in the basement.

Few more important propositions could be advanced at the present time, since large numbers of people all over the world are arriving at the same conclusion. The question is, how are we going to use this freedom? Freedom is both a privilege and a danger of terrifying proportions. Again, one is reminded of the fourteenth century and its huge, collective premonition of a final ending: a universal climax. Of course, what the fourteenth century didn't realise, as it gloomed over its skeleton dances, was that the electric springtime of the Renaissance was just around the corner – to produce Alberti, who said: 'Man can do all things, if he will.' Most of us reserve a wry smile for that statement now; but Colin Wilson would agree with Alberti wholeheartedly. This is refreshing; and in fact he's prophesying a new renaissance. But this renaissance, as the mystics have been prophesying all along, is within us: a renaissance of spiritual power.

Having produced evidence for the existence of precognition, spirits, witchcraft, life after death, and unplumbed powers in man and nature, Wilson sums up by saying that we are enmeshed in a misconception about our own nature; that we see ourselves as 'helpless creatures, born into a universe we fail to understand'. Untrue, he says; the evidence of paranormal research shows that there is a part of our being that knows far more than our conscious mind; and we may 'know' even greater secrets than this. It's Wilson's thesis that the nineteenth-century Romantics, and the 'outsiders' who descended from them, began to plumb these secrets; and by this I take him to mean that Wordsworth's vision of immortality in childhood was no pretty fancy, but an actual, remembered vision of another life, with which we tragically lose touch. But this realisation of the Romantics, Wilson contends, was intuitive, lacking in confidence, and led to the Romantic despair; the modern vision of the artist who is impotent in his freedom – a freedom that destroys him. Hence the agonies of Shelley; Wagner; Rimbaud. Such artists marked a new stage in consciousness, but in Wilson's view, didn't go far enough. Nor did they go away; there are millions of Romantics today, and Romanticism, with its emphasis on private vision and private fantasy, is the dominant outlook of the century.

What Wilson doesn't discuss much in all this is the possible role of a personal creator; and he admits that his conclusions bring us 'alarmingly close to the world-view of our ancestors: a completely irrational world where anything can happen'. He does at one point refer to the fact that a mystic would see God 'at the top of the ladder of selves'; and one might be inclined to see this as the missing key in Wilson's puzzle. But leaving that aside, perhaps we ought to be looking fairly closely at what it will be like to return to 'a completely irrational world where anything can happen'.

If paganism returns, in whatever resplendent new gear it puts on for the occasion, how will this affect us? Maybe we should take time to remember what it was like back there, as the new worshippers of the earth from middle-class suburbs go happily to their power-places in the bush, reinstating the old festivals, summoning the Old Ones of Europe from distant highways of sky – or here in Australia, invoking the spirits that only the Aboriginals knew, which hide in special rocks and thickets. At night in the bush, they listen for the Mapooram. I have heard and thrilled to it myself. But should we listen too long?

History never truly repeats itself, and it would be naive to assume that a new paganism will exactly reproduce the scenarios of the old. Nevertheless, some similar features seem likely to occur; and the best point from which to look back on the paganism that was replaced by Christendom is probably the fifth century AD, when the Roman Empire was completing its infinitely slow collapse. The fifth century is a sort of black hole in time, and not many theorists have taken an interest in it. One

who did was Frédéric Ozanam, Professor of Foreign Literature at the Sorbonne, and a leading Catholic intellectual in
nineteenth-century France: the founder of the Society of St
Vincent de Paul. An inheritor of the Enlightenment, he de-
picted the turning point that led from paganism to Christianity
with didactic intent, since his purpose was to confront the
strongly anti-Christian positions of his own day; tendencies
born out of the French Revolution. His book, *A History of
Civilization in the Fifth Century*, has a tone of embattled,
sometimes unctuous piety that grows off-putting to the contemporary ear. But his partisan criticism of paganism perhaps
has a certain interest in the present period, which is accepting
its return so uncritically.

Ozanam reminds the reader of the obvious fact that the
pagan world rested on slavery – which Christendom rejected –
and he goes on to outline what this meant. It meant human
beings as objects for use, with all the physical and sexual abuse
that followed. It meant a contempt for human life so profound
that a father could expose his child at birth. It meant human
sacrifice – and not just in Rome's early days. In 'the brightest
age of the republic and the empire', a male and female Gaul
and a pair of Greeks were buried alive to avert the prediction of
an oracle which had promised Rome to the barbarians. Pliny
was impressed only by the majesty of the ceremony. And
Ozanam tells the story of Alypius, a friend of St Augustine, who
was a philosopher and a man of great refinement. He went one
day against his better judgement to the Circus, which he said
he loathed, vowing to keep his eyes closed. But when he heard
the death-shrieks he opened them, and ended by shouting for
blood with the most ardent of the mob; and he became, from
then on, addicted to the cruelty of the arena. It would be facile

to draw too close a parallel with our own time; but we do seem to have grown more and more fond of blood in our films in the last two decades; and now we have 'snuff movies' where unwitting prostitutes are butchered at the end of the show. The Romans would have appreciated that; they did it in the theatre.

Ozanam's theme is that the crude Christendom which replaced sophisticated Rome – the rough, violent world of the Franks and Goths – had one overriding new virtue that sprang peculiarly from Christianity: respect for the uniqueness and immortality of the person as a child of God; a liberating reverence for the human spirit. 'Self respect,' Ozanam says, 'was present in every hovel.' Broken many times, disgraced, even half-drowned in blood, the ideal nevertheless prevailed: St Augustine's City of God did replace the city of hedonism and cruelty. Christian Europe, despite its wars and its tortures, didn't feature the arena, or blood sacrifice, or forced euthanasia.

Christendom, with its accompanying ideal of chivalry, has of course become a museum-piece since Ozanam's book was written. It probably received its *coup de grâce* from the Nazis – who were not really an end-product of Christian Europe at all, but among the first of the new pagans. Despising both Christianity and Judaism, the Nazi leaders were deeply involved with secret occult ceremonies: intent on bringing back the old Norse gods to replace the Judaeo-Christian ethic of love and mercy which they saw as enfeebled and enfeebling. Certainly that ethic and belief is enfeebled today – despised by intellectuals on the one hand and fantastically vulgarised, distorted and exploited by TV evangelists on the other. And the position of a novelist holding Christian beliefs is very unfashionable indeed, since Christianity alone among current ideologies is fair game for ridicule: the clown of the belief-systems.

In writing for an audience of mixed beliefs, an author of Christian conviction (and one of orthodox Jewish conviction too, no doubt) must tread the soft pedal where his or her values are concerned. This is to some extent reasonable; a novelist's job is to interpret and speak to his time, and he can scarcely do that carrying fixed messages from beyond reality to which his audience is not receptive. He has no business seeking to proselytise or convert, since when propaganda comes in the door, art goes out the window; but his position is made difficult when he cannot assume common values with his audience at all – not even the Judaeo-Christian position that a master like Tolstoy took up. Tolstoy was living in a period whose spiritual condition was similar to ours: large numbers of the Russian young were rejecting family, religion and all social institutions, there was an epidemic of suicides, and Tolstoy contemplated suicide himself. But what marks the crucial difference between his era and ours is the nature of the hard-won Christian conviction that finally lifted him out of his impasse. This conviction, which his readers found neither unacceptable nor naive, was highly individual, since Tolstoy ended by rejecting the Russian Orthodox Church of his childhood; yet it is finally within the mainstream of Christian optimism. And it is this optimism – his belief that all will be well if God is known and trusted – combined with a sternly uncompromising spirit and a formidable intellectual restlessness, as impressive now as they were to his contemporaries, that make him stand in such contrast to the serious writers of today.

Having searched the hypotheses and conclusions of the important European thinkers, from Plato to Hegel, from

Socrates to Schopenhauer, he had found in all of them little more than a message of resignation about the futility of life. But then came the revelation from which he never afterwards wavered. 'I turned my eyes,' he wrote, 'to the huge masses of simple, ignorant, poor people, and I saw something altogether different.' These people, he saw, drew their courage and vitality and acceptance of the world from a very simple faith; and Tolstoy wrote in his notebook: 'As soon as man applies his intelligence and only his intelligence to any object at all, he unfailingly destroys the object.' One spring day, walking in the forest, it was borne in on him that he always felt sad when he rejected God with his reason, and was always cheerful when he accepted him like a child. 'The moment I thought I knew God,' he wrote, 'I lived. To know God and to live are the same thing.' The fruits of this spiritual odyssey, it will be remembered, appear in *War and Peace*; and in the chapter towards the end where Pierre Bezuhov looks into the mirror of faith, we experience the serene joy expressed by the mind on finding its natural home; a joy whose flavour recalls that of a Bach cantata.

... he flung aside the telescope through which he had hitherto been gazing over men's heads, and looked joyfully at the ever-changing, ever grand, unfathomable and infinite life about him. And the closer he looked at it, the calmer and happier he was. The terrible question that had shattered all his intellectual edifices in the old days, the question: *What for?* had no existence for him now. To that question, *What for?* he had now always ready in his soul the simple answer: because there is a God, that God without whom not one hair of a man's head falls.

To contrast this with a passage from Graham Greene – one which is also a declaration of faith – is very revealing in what it has to show about our two centuries, and the different nature of their spirits. I am referring to the haunting statement from *The Lawless Roads*.

> And so faith came to one – shapelessly, without dogma, a presence above the croquet lawn, something associated with violence, cruelty, evil, across the way. One began to believe in heaven because one believed in hell, but for a long while it was only hell one could picture with a certain intimacy . . .

Faith in our time, for one of the most important novelists the century has produced, came as a sort of illness, and was unaccompanied by optimism; and those characters in Greene's novels who possess faith harbour it like a cancer, like a grand penalty – something that will lead them into situations more terrible than faith's absence. The characters of Dostoevsky inhabit a world as grim as many of Greene's do, and consequences fall on them with the same chilling inevitability; but even inside the horror at the end of *Crime and Punishment* there is the same optimism as Tolstoy's: a knowledge of salvation that is joyful as well as terrible, and which makes our current spiritual condition look somehow shrunken. Despite his murder of the old pawnbroker woman, Raskolnikov will not be denied redemption; and the scene where he is shown the way to it by the prostitute Sonia would never be dared by a contemporary writer, who would be branded as wildly melodramatic if he even attempted it. Yet read it with a truthful heart, and you know that such an exchange is not only possible, but is still bound to be happening in the world.

'But it was the devil that killed that old woman, not I. Enough, Sonia, enough! Let me be!' he cried, in a sudden spasm of agony. 'Let me be!'

He leaned his elbows on his knees and squeezed his head in his hands as in a vice.

'What suffering!' A wail of anguish broke from Sonia.

'Well, what am I to do now?' he asked.

'What are you to do?' she cried, jumping up; and her eyes that had been full of tears suddenly began to shine. 'Stand up!' She seized him by the shoulder, and he got up, looking at her almost bewildered. 'Go at once, this very minute, stand at the crossroads, bow down, first kiss the earth which you have defiled and then bow down to all the world and say to all men aloud, "I am a murderer!" Then God will send you life again. Will you go, will you go?'

Despite the wave of revolution that was poised to break over it, Russia was then a predominantly Christian country, and Dostoevsky could be sure of his audience's response to a scene like this: sure of shared belief in the consequences of sin and the certainty of salvation for the repentant. A contemporary writer can be certain of no such certainties; and all that a Christian novelist can reasonably do in these circumstances is to place some characters among his cast who are Christian, and whose hungers and conflicts are governed by that fact. But it would seem quite likely, since ours is increasingly an era of conflicting spiritual beliefs, and of an overt return to sorcery and 'white magic', that the task of the novelist generally, in the decades ahead, may be to reflect a Titanic struggle between forces of good and ill in the human psyche. Such a volatile spiritual situation as this half of our century presents ought surely to be of special interest to the writer. Jonestown ought to be of interest; and the cults that are sacrificing babies in the woods; and the phenomenon of Carlos Castaneda – that peculiar graduate student from the University of California who openly advocates sophisticated witchcraft as an ethic and a way of life, and whose books sell in millions.

Plainly, the message transmitted by Castaneda in particular is not to be taken lightly. Nor is it, by distinguished critics. The *New Statesman* has announced that 'if Castaneda really witnessed the events he describes, this is a fact of extraordinary importance for mankind.' And the *Sunday Times* has said: 'These books may be the *Pilgrim's Progress* of our time.'

If they are, it's worth trying to fathom what new rewards the hopeful pilgrim is being led towards.

I have read a number of Castaneda's books with interest. They drew me in as they have drawn so many others. But the pilgrimage, despite the remarkable phenomena and the moments of thrilling alarm and the mind-altering occurrences and challenges to the self along the way, out there in the Mexican desert, required in the end a certain patience. In fact, despite all the portentousness that the books do so much to build up, they began to accumulate an atmosphere the name of which is tedium.

For a time, I thought this tedium was brought about by my own impatience; I wanted to know the secrets too soon. But in the end, I realised that it was not manufactured by me at all; nor by Castaneda himself. Nor was it a tedium resulting from flagging power to interest. No; this was a very special and paradoxical tedium: *one where interest and curiosity were still constantly present.* Anyone who's experienced this tedium will know what it's like. It's what Mick Jagger was singing about in

'Satisfaction'. It's the longing for a sweet and satisfying drink, held just beyond reach when thirst is tormenting. It's a tedium that promises ecstasy, and yet holds terror and despair at its centre – the tedium of which Baudelaire wrote:

> Though it makes no great gesture, no great cry,
> It would lay waste the earth quite willingly,
> And in a yawn engulf creation.

Castaneda's books (for those who don't know them) relate the story of his apprenticeship to the old Yaqui Indian sorcerer don Juan Matus, in order to become a sorcerer himself. Don Juan leads the bemused Castaneda through sensation after sensation and dialogue after dialogue aimed at an enlightenment which is power. These are the arts of the warrior, he says, gained through experiences either induced by peyote or mushrooms or else by the special disciplines that make such stimulants unnecessary. Don Juan is an engaging, sardonic and even amusing figure. (I almost said endearing; but no, he is never endearing. As with all sorcerers, his humour and his gestures at closeness are entirely without warmth.) But he is also often threatening, and so are the experiences beyond the normal he induces. Time and again, Castaneda describes himself as being terrified – not just by the things he sees, and his altered perception of the world, but by don Juan himself.

> He signalled me with his eyes. I turned and I thought I saw a flickering movement over the boulder. A chill ran through my body . . . and I experienced a jolt, a spasm . . .
>
> 'Death is our eternal companion,' don Juan said with a most serious air . . . 'It has always been watching you. It always will until the day it taps you.'

He extended his arm and touched me lightly on the shoulder and at the same time he made a deep clicking sound with his tongue. The effect was devastating; I almost got sick to my stomach.

A warrior, don Juan says (by which he means a sorcerer), seeks power; 'and one of the avenues to power is dreaming.' Dreaming is real, don Juan says; and throughout the long journey to revelation, it's constantly emphasised for Castaneda that the warrior will actually enter this other dimension, and that he will do it alone, having been aided by dangerous spirit 'allies'. The warrior is thus coldly self-sufficient, outside normal reality, and hunts power. It is emphasised that he will be above all pettiness; and it is hinted that great peace and calm will result from self-mastery: the end-product of all transcendental quests.

Yet what seems curiously at odds with this level of wisdom is that don Juan and his fellow-sorcerer don Genaro constantly wish to physically frighten Castaneda (for his own enlightenment, apparently), and that these two supremely wise masters have a remarkable fondness for obscene and ugly tricks, either in words or deeds: tricks which are essentially petty, infantile, and at the same time sinister.

'Genaro is going to tell you something,' don Juan said to me all of a sudden.

. . . Don Genaro looked at me and contracted his lips until his mouth looked like a round hole. He curled his tongue against his palate and opened and closed his mouth as if he were having spasms.

'Look, look at his mouth. That's the hen's ass and it is about to lay an egg.'

The two constantly alternate between encouragement and mockery: a strange and incongruous activity in enlightened men. And in *Tales of Power*, just before Castaneda comes to the climactic moment to which all his pilgrimage has been leading – 'the sorcerer's explanation' which will see his breaking through into the supreme level of dream – he is led into an experience that so terrifies and distresses him that he literally shits himself, while the two sorcerers howl with laughter.

> I saw instantly a good-size rock tumbling down the wall of the ravine towards me. In a flash I also saw don Genaro throwing it. I had an attack of panic . . . I looked around. Don Juan began to laugh and said that don Genaro had left because he could not stand my stench.

Fear; filth; infantile mockery: a curious and repellent accompaniment to ultimate spiritual enlightenment; a curious initiation! Such attitudes and activities don't accompany the insights brought to us by the spiritual masters of the higher religions. They are not the attributes of that truth which enlarges the spirit and fills it with love; not the face of that love which frees us from fear, and which every mystic has told us accompanies true union with God.

But union with God and love of humankind with all humankind's frailties, is not, as far as one can discover, what don Juan is offering; he is offering 'the sorcerer's explanation', which is power: power drawn from within the self, and from within the earth.

> 'The antidote that kills that poison is here,' don Juan said, caressing the ground. 'The sorcerer's explanation cannot at

all liberate the spirit . . . Only the love for this splendorous being can give freedom to a warrior's spirit; and freedom is joy, efficiency, and abandon in the face of any odds . . . The twilight is the crack between the worlds . . . It is the door to the unknown.'

He pointed with a sweeping movement of his hand to the mesa where we were standing.

'There is the door. Beyond, there is an abyss and beyond that abyss is the unknown.'

This final message has an overt attractiveness; it speaks of joy. But joy is not convincingly shown to accompany it. What accompanies it, standing in the shadows, is fear, and paganism's old bogies: the shapes of formless menace, the power of the unseen, and beyond that, 'the abyss'.

It's interesting to place this book beside one of the last great novels in this century by an orthodox Catholic: Georges Bernanos' *The Diary of a Country Priest*. There are striking parallels and contrasts.

In the first place, Bernanos' novel also concerns itself with tedium: that amorphous and terrible creature which always dogs our footsteps, and from which, as Colin Wilson contends, it's our most important spiritual task to escape. Here is don Juan on tedium:

'That dog's barking is the nocturnal voice of man,' don Juan said . . . 'That barking and the loneliness it creates, speaks of the feelings of men . . . for whom an entire life was like one Sunday afternoon . . .

'That afternoon left them only with the memory of petty annoyance and tedium, and then suddenly it was over; it was already night.'

Bernanos, in his novel, begins by portraying just this tedium, in a depressed and almost hopeless world: a world of grey poverty in the French provinces, beset by illness and petty evil. The young priest writes in his diary:

My parish is bored stiff; no other word for it. Like so many others! We can see them being eaten up by boredom . . . You can keep going a long time with that in you.

A miserable parish; a small priest of peasant origin dying of stomach cancer, who feels he is failing his people. Yet as the diary goes on, it's not tedium that permeates the book, but extraordinary joy, as the priest is revealed inexorably to be a saint. His passionate love of God spreads and glows through the account until squalor gives way to formidable light. His timidity hides the strength of faith; his stubborn concern and love transform the lives of all those he involves himself with. Like St Francis, he's a fool for God, and his wretched death is a triumph. For Bernanos, tedium and evil are terrifying and negative forces, to be resisted without cease; and they cannot in the end overcome goodness. Goodness is not only more dynamic than evil; it's revealed in the most unexpected places – even in squalor. Perhaps especially in squalor, as the country priest seems to be demonstrating. He makes the comfortable bourgeoisie of his parish uneasy, since his faith is uncompromising and revolutionary, just as Christ's was; just as the Incarnation itself was: a revolutionary fact shaking reality forever, bringing joy to those who wish to accept it.

If there is one word that characterises Bernanos' dark and anguished world, it's joy: a joy that isn't named like a talisman, as it is in Castaneda's work, but which emerges out of pain with a truth that can't be mistaken. The word is used like a hammer by the old Curé de Torcy, the young priest's mentor, who seems also to be speaking of that abyss named by don Juan.

'If I could get hold of one of those learned gents who say I obscure the truth, I'd tell him! I'd say: I can't help wearing an outfit like an undertaker's man. After all, the Pope rigs himself up in white and the cardinals in red, so what's the odds? But I'd have the right to go round adorned like the queen of Sheba because I'm bringing you joy. I'll give it you for nothing, you have only to ask. Joy is the gift of the Church, whatever joy is possible for this sad world to share. Whatever you did against the Church has been done against joy.

'What would it profit you even to create life itself, when you have lost all sense of what life really is? Manufacture "life" as much as you like, I say! It's the vision you give us of death that poisons the thoughts of poor devils . . .

'But just you wait. Wait for the first quarter of an hour's silence. Then the Word will be heard of men – not the voice they rejected, which spoke so quietly: "I am the Way, the Resurrection, and the Life" – but the voice from the depths: "I am the door for ever locked, the road which leads nowhere, the lie, the everlasting dark."'

And in the young priest's diary the darkness is pushed back in the midst of his illness with a certainty that resembles Tolstoy's:

How little we know what a human life really is – even our own. To judge us by what we call our actions is probably as futile as to judge us by our dreams. God's justice chooses from this dark conglomeration of thought and act, and that which is raised towards the Father shines with a sudden burst of light, displayed in glory like a sun.

This is all that a Christian novelist can do, in the end: to salvage joy wherever it's to be found, among the rubbish and waste and pathetic incongruities of life; and to show as well the results of its displacement; to identify those counterfeits that come to us in its place, whispering their lies of fulfilment, power and love.

Such a novelist will tend, in weaving his fantasies, to recall St Augustine's words, addressed to God: 'In darkened affections is the true distance from thy face.'

# The Novel as Narrative Poem

*A Personal View*

I

How many people today read Thomas Wolfe? Not many, I suspect. But Wolfe, a contemporary of Scott Fitzgerald and William Faulkner, had a reputation in his day at least as big as theirs, and even more success in terms of acclaim and sales.

Those who have read him will be familiar with his faults – the overwriting, the prolixity, the sheer inability to control his mass of material. If ever a writer was drunk with words, Wolfe was, and his legend makes him seem larger than life: a giant of a man from the rural South, prowling the streets of New York at night, trying to absorb every impression the city had to give, and by day pouring it out in thousands of words; a man who wanted, like Proust, to fix forever every youthful memory; who wanted to read every good book ever written, and who never lost the dreams of adolescence, before his tragic early death at thirty-eight. For all his excesses, Wolfe was a genius: a poet who chose to write in prose and became one of the great prose-poets of the century, but whose virtues are a novelist's virtues, his characters rivalling those of Dickens in their sheer vitality.

He's the Walt Whitman of the novel. No one set down the whole richness, beauty and sadness of America as he did. His is an eagle's view of the continent, and he lays it all out before us in haunting detail: the great cities, the small towns, the deserts and the forest and the wastelands: America the beautiful, in that great period between the Civil War and World War II, before some of the dream went sour. Wolfe's vision and his incredible memory have captured forever the smallest sights and sounds of that America: the look of a row of freight cars on a siding; the blue ridges of Carolina; the clopping of a milkman's horse at dawn, in a little town in the South.

It was Thomas Wolfe who caused me to become a writer. One has to lay blame for this calamity somewhere, and so one turns to those influences of very early youth, just beyond the bounds of childhood: those writers who carried one away, who said things that one had never believed anyone else could feel, let alone say. 'Could I make tongue say more than tongue could utter!' This was the grand task Wolfe had set himself; and reading him with the ecstasies we only know at sixteen, I believed that he had done it:

> Remembering speechlessly we seek the great forgotten language, the lost lane-end into heaven, a stone, a leaf, an unfound door. Where? When?
>
> O lost, and by the wind grieved, ghost, come back again.

No one, it seemed to me, had ever written of these secret things before.

Graham Greene, in 'The Lost Childhood', has said that it's childhood reading that has the deepest influence on our lives. Later in life we may admire greater literature, we may have better taste and discrimination; but never again will we know the intense excitement of those first revelations in print. This was how it was for me with Wolfe; and above all, he showed me what the novel could be: that it could do far more than tell a story; that it could weave the poetry of my world; my time.

Now that I'm older, I can see Wolfe's technical faults. I can regret his inability to learn restraint; to synthesise, to plan. But what do these things matter beside his exultant celebration of the beauty and mystery of the world? No other writer will give

me what he gave me, if only because the experience of which he
wrote so uncannily corresponded to my own. A boy growing up
in the cool hills of North Carolina in the early years of this
century, dreaming of the great cities in the North that he would
some day discover; a boy listening at night to the lonely cry of
the train that would one day take him there: this was what
Wolfe wrote of. And these things miraculously matched the
dreams of a boy listening to the train-cry in the cool hills of
Tasmania in the 1940s, imagining unknown cities on the
mainland of Australia he would one day see. I don't doubt that
Wolfe's evocation of longing and promise matched the experience and the dreams of country boys and small town boys
everywhere; but few writers in this country then gave them
utterance. Wonder and joy, the vision of optimism and
innocence, came to me from the northern hemisphere:

Trains cross the continent in a swirl of dust and thunder, the
leaves fly down the tracks behind them: the great trains
cleave through gulch and gulley, they rumble with spoked
thunder on the bridges . . . they whip past empty stations in
the little towns and their great stride pounds its even pulse
across America.

. . . And the great winds howl and swoop across the land:
they make a distant roaring in great trees, and boys in bed
will stir in ecstasy, thinking of demons and vast swoopings
through the earth . . .

And often in the night there is only the living silence, the
distant frosty barking of a dog, the small clumsy stir and
feathery stumble of the chickens on limed roosts, and the
moon, the low and heavy moon of autumn, now barred
behind the leafless poles of pines, now at the pinewood's

brooding edge and summit, now falling with ghost's dawn of
milky light upon rimed clods of fields . . .

Back in the 1930s, in the age of the train and the steamship,
before television, when the novel was king, Wolfe found a
whole generation to respond to his American canvas and his
exultant adolescent dreams. He was a bestseller not only in
America but in Britain, and in the Germany of his paternal
ancestors; and he was idolised by the young. He found a
response to his dense, exuberant, romantic prose on a scale
that I think might not be possible today. But in the 1950s, still
in the pre-television age, when I began to write, such a thing
was still possible: we were still a civilisation where words were
paramount. And so I chose to write novels, with the same naive
belief in the future that Wolfe had known.

I had begun by writing verse; but at nineteen, I already knew
that the novel was my first love. The reasons then were obvious:
everything one wanted to say could be said in the novel; I could
try, as Wolfe had tried, to tell what had never quite been told, to
chart that dream-country which we all carry within us, and
which, unattended, will dwindle on the horizon and disappear.
And as well as this, I could hope for an audience not in
hundreds, but in tens of thousands. Unless one failed
altogether, it seemed almost a certainty, in those days: even a
mediocre novel could count on a healthy sale. And I still
believe, grandiose and egotistical though this hope may now
appear, that it was an honourable hope. To reach into the
hearts and secret lives of ordinary men and women, not just of a
supposedly cultivated few, and to do it by communicating the
best one had, not the worst, not the spurious, not the concocted
– what real writer wouldn't want this?

The process of evolution that had brought me to novel-writing had as its first phase a childhood ambition that was somewhat more crude: I wanted to be a comic-strip artist. From the age of eight I had worked at drawing my own comic strips with a fanatic's persistence. I was determined to produce strip cartoons like 'Felix the Cat', 'The Phantom', 'Ginger Meggs' and 'Wanda the War Girl'; and although I spent time with books as well, my most serious attention was given to the comics. I studied them; and I can still recite the names of the artists and writers who produced all the major American and Australian strips of the day. In that pre-television era, they had much more glamour than they do now, and I informed my dubious parents that the rewards of being a Pat Sullivan, a Lee Falk, a Jim Bancks or a Kate O'Brien could be dazzling. The fact is, I suppose, that I already wanted to tell stories; and by doing so within my set of strip-cartoon frames I could escape for a time from the thought of school, which I detested.

At the age of fifteen, in third-year high school, still drawing comics, I managed to fail in every subject except English. It was decided that I was more or less subnormal; and since I liked reading so much, I was put to work in a bookshop, where I found myself sweeping floors, carrying parcels and occasionally serving customers.

This Dickensian experience put some iron into my soul, and I realised that I was destined to become a failure. But the bookshop had an ancient basement, and I began to escape down there and read the stock. I discovered Thomas Wolfe and James Joyce; trembling with lust and horror, I devoured the Molly Bloom sequence in *Ulysses*: strong meat for a Catholic boy in the 1940s. I read Dostoevsky, Hemingway, Thomas Mann, D. H. Lawrence; most of the great nineteenth-

and twentieth-century novelists. And I began to neglect my comic-strip drawing, because I'd now begun to suspect that the novel could be the supreme comic strip.

Unfortunately, these joys were brought to an end by old Mr Fuller, the bookshop proprietor, who discovered me reading in the basement; and not just in the basement, but in his own little den down there, where he entertained publishers' agents with scotch, and kept his library of rare editions and soft pornography. He fired me.

We usually get what we want a little too late, and at this point I became an apprentice press artist and cartoonist on the Hobart *Mercury*, where I lasted about a year. But my heart wasn't in it. I was going to be a writer: I wanted to read, not work, so I went back to school, and then on to university. There I discovered not only world literature, but Australian poetry. Those of us with a literary bent read our favourite poets each week in the old Sydney *Bulletin* – then the one important platform for Australian writers – and my friend Vivian Smith and I had our own first poems accepted there. Poets such as Kenneth Slessor, David Campbell, David Rowbotham, Roland Robinson and Judith Wright had shown us that Australia could be interpreted and transfigured.

But the novelists who influenced me were all, like Thomas Wolfe, from the countries of the other hemisphere. I had searched in vain for a Eugene Gant or a Raskolnikov or a Lord Jim or a Captain Ahab in Australian fiction: those characters of complex nature who hurled themselves at life in hope or despair; who made huge demands of it. And I had no use for the strange idea that we should make allowances for our early fiction, or support it patriotically. We had produced a great poem like 'Five Bells'; why hadn't we produced a *Moby Dick*? I couldn't arrive at an answer then. Now, at the distance of three decades, I can hazard a few theories.

In Australia, we differed from Americans like Wolfe in one particular. Wolfe's was a vision not only of a haunting rural past, but of the golden city of success: of a shining paradise in New York that could actually be reached by any young man or woman with hope and talent: the old American dream. But there wasn't an equivalent Australian dream. Ours was an often pessimistic and sardonic country, where material success was looked on with suspicion and the shining city was just a mirage, out in the sand.

That isn't surprising, if one contrasts the two experiences of European settlement. When the American pioneers pushed into the interior of that continent, they found the Mississippi valley – one of the most beautiful and abundant regions on earth. They found the great plains. Our pioneers pushed into the interior expecting an inland sea, since British geographers reasoned that no continent could be as dry as this one appeared. They speculated that a new Mediterranean, the source of many of the rivers, lay hidden beyond the deserts in the centre; and Captain Charles Sturt – whose journal is a classic of our early literature – was so confident that he would find the sea that his expedition of 1844 carried a boat through the desert. But the creeks dried up behind them and in front of them; the thermometer recorded 132° Fahrenheit in the shade and then burst; and at Milparinka, the party was trapped beside a water hole for six months waiting for rain, 'as effectually,' Sturt wrote, 'as though we had wintered at the pole.'

They then pressed on with their terrible trek (a journey that in the end totalled 3000 miles), through heat that caused leaves to fall from the trees and the birds to die; through appalling

deserts of gibber stones; through territories empty of any life
but the ant, until they had actually come to the heart of the
continent: the region of desolation now called the Simpson
Desert. It was here that Sturt saw the truth, and even his
optimism gave out. Let his journal tell the rest.

> From the summit of a sandy undulation . . . we saw that the
> ridges extended northwards in parallel lines beyond the
> range of vision . . . like the waves of the sea. The sand was of
> a deep red colour . . . My companion involuntarily uttered an
> exclamation when he glanced his eye over it. 'Good
> Heavens,' said he, 'did man ever see such a country!'

There was no inland sea; only more desert. No bread, but
gibber stones. There is a grand pathos in Sturt's expedition,
and in that useless boat. The sea that wasn't there has taunted
the Australian soul ever since; and despite the temperate
beauties and fertility of our eastern and southern seaboards,
we've been suspicious since then of paradise on earth, and of
easy answers. And our novelists have lately tended to look for
the dream-country in less tangible zones.

They didn't always do so. While Australia produced remarkable poets between the turn of the century and the 1950s –
poets who explored the world of the invisible as well as the
actual – our prose writers for the most part were realists of the
most dispiriting kind, devoted to a sort of glum and passionless
social documentation. It was as though the physical hazards and
discouragements of Australia – the droughts and crop failures
and the unseen fact of the desert at its heart – had affected their
spirits like a blight. This even permeates one of the most
impressive novels of the period, Henry Handel Richardson's
*The Fortunes of Richard Mahony*. There were exceptions, of

course – notably Hal Porter, who had been producing his vital, ornate and pitiless prose poems on urban and small town Australia since the 1930s; and Richardson herself had written the finest novel of passion in our literature: *Maurice Guest.* But significantly, this was set in Europe.

One can advance possible reasons for this ascendancy of verse over fiction until recently. A poet synthesises and compresses experience rather than charting its details, constructing inner as well as outer landscapes. A novelist can't limit himself to this; landscape, and the essence of experience may concern him too, but he must also be concerned with society itself. Our history has been blessedly free of extremes – untouched by civil wars, revolutions, or invasions. But perhaps if a society lacks extremes of despair or joy, great novels aren't likely.

There is also an absence of the transcendental in early Australian novels. Hunger for God is absent, and a flat materialism holds them down. In Christina Stead's *For Love Alone*, this hunger does appear, surfacing as paganism: her young heroine, Teresa, maddened by the emptiness and frustration of her life in Sydney, longs for the return of Aphrodite. 'Venus,' she pleads, 'what am I to do? No one will help me.' This is the prose equivalent of Kenneth Slessor's call for a migration of the Greek gods and nature spirits to the environs of Sydney: the 'new Athens' in the southern hemisphere that the painter Norman Lindsay had envisaged.

> This garden by the dark Lane Cove
> Shall spark before thy music dies
> With silver sandals; all the gods
> Be conjured from Ionian skies.

> Those poplars in a fluting-trice
> They'll charm into an olive grove
> And dance a while in Paradise
> Like men of fire above Lane Cove.

Today, Australia is becoming a more cosmopolitan, complex, difficult and therefore less dull society, and is possibly entering the major phase of its evolution as a nation. But my generation remember that terrible lack of possibilities, that empty suburban silence that maddened poor Teresa in her stifling little room at Watson's Bay, and drove so many writers like Christina Stead and Shirley Hazzard and Randolph Stow overseas in their youth. It drove me away too. I'd fallen in love with the landscape of my native Tasmania; but this wasn't enough to hold me.

The big change for our fiction began in the mid-fifties, at the time when I was finishing my first novel in London. I had sat in a tiny bedsitter in Notting Hill Gate for something like eighteen months, in the evenings after work in various jobs, writing about a world 12,000 miles away, in Tasmania and Melbourne; now, at the end of 1956, I left the manuscript with an agent and sailed for home. *The Boys in the Island* was a young novel, with most of the faults and crudities of youth; but I believed it to be different from the novels then appearing in Australia. I was soon to find that I was wrong.

In the week of my departure from Britain, I discovered Patrick White's newly published novel *The Tree of Man* in a bookshop in Charing Cross Road; and in 1958, when *The Boys in the Island* finally found publication, Randolph Stow's *To the Islands* appeared. Both of these novels were doing what I most valued in fiction: they were charting inward journeys, not just outward ones: their authors were prepared to bring to the novel the methods of poetry, and to deal with irrational and mysterious impulses in the human psyche. I wasn't alone; and it delighted me.

Vincent Buckley, in an article written some time later called 'In the Shadow of Patrick White', linked Stow and me to White, and claimed that a new direction in Australian fiction had been established through White's influence. Neither Stow nor I had read White's work when we wrote our own novels; but Buckley's article was still true in its essential perception. There are mysterious underground springs in literature that can surface at the same time in different places.

2

A lot has happened since the fifties. Since that decade, those dreams of vast audiences have had to be watered down a little, since the novel is no longer king. The largest audiences available today are for the young man or woman who becomes a film director – or better still, that hybrid creature most feared by screenwriters, an *auteur* director. But I'm not about to launch into an elegy on the decline of the novel. In my opinion it isn't greatly declining, nor will it; and in fact, the rewards in terms of sales and reputation can still be great. But it now occupies second place, as far as the mass audience is concerned, to the visual media – and that's a peculiar place to occupy, carrying with it different stresses. Both as an art form and as a popular form, the novel is now in a new situation. I believe it's a situation that has caused some distortions, and a certain loss of confidence: but I also believe that the novelist's basic task hasn't greatly changed, and that the road to success in fiction – success, that is, in communicating with an audience of consequence – remains the same road.

What has happened is that the novel has split and polarised, and the middle ground of fiction is threatened. The gap between the commercial blockbuster and the novel that has more serious aims has been widening; and that's somewhat dangerous to the general well-being of the novel. Pleasure in the actual sound and cadence of prose and pleasure in words themselves seems somewhat diminished lately, both for those who write novels and those who read them. There have been few recent novelists in English who create this pleasure. We have novelists now of great sophistication in their social and cultural concerns: novelists with all sorts of ironical messages and drums to beat, and an abundance of what continues somewhat tediously to be called 'black humour'; but it's hard to find an equivalent to the verbal beauties of Joyce, Thomas Mann, Wolfe, Forster, Fitzgerald, Greene, Faulkner or Lawrence Durrell; rare to find those moments that create a response in which crucial, sympathetic emotion and aesthetic pleasure are perfectly fused. This is partly because orchestration is absent from a good many contemporary novels: that attention to the kind of structure, counterpoint, and the action of symbolic themes which can make fiction approach music: the echo and enigma in the Marabar caves and the reappearance of the wasp, in *A Passage to India*; the sanatorium which is mortally sick Europe in *The Magic Mountain*; the river at whose source is the spirit's barbarism in *Heart of Darkness*; the light on Daisy's dock in *The Great Gatsby* – whose wonderful last paragraph rises with inevitable power to become an elegiac poem about the whole heartbreak of time and loss and our longing for the impossible.

Such novels, mostly written in the early decades of this century, took the fiction form beyond the knockabout narrative of the eighteenth and early nineteenth centuries and brought it to a new level of art, hitherto the province of verse and music. And in my view, they effectively established the novel as the successor to narrative poetry in this century.

I'm not saying that the novel can replace the lyric poem. Nothing can do that, since lyric poetry's heightened utterance springs from the tension of its brevity, from the verse form itself, and from the sort of compression that results in pure song. But verse as narrative, or even verse exposition of a theme, has become limited and above all artificial by contrast with the novel. Narrative poetry simply can't build as the novel can build; it can't (without unbearable tedium) portray character and destiny by that inexorable accumulation of small moments and minute observations which approximate life itself, and become in the end major revelations. It can't, in other words, compete as either a storytelling form or as a form that reproduces life's patterning; and its own advantage over fiction was long ago lost, since the novel, in addition to its supremacy as narrative, has now shown that it can do everything poetry can do, outside the magic circle of the lyric. *The Divine Comedy* and *Paradise Lost* would today be written as novels; and now that the visual media can present straightforward narrative so much more vividly than fiction, the novel as narrative poem seems to me the only form of fiction worth pursuing.

But perhaps I should make a little clearer what I mean by 'the novel as narrative poem', since the term 'poetic novel' is lately used all too easily and loosely – often being applied to works which are merely decorative in their expression, and which don't have the attributes I'm speaking of. 'Poetic novel' has an unfortunate flavour of arty pretentiousness; but then, the term 'novel' itself is pretty silly and inexact, as well as being inadequate to describe the varied types of fiction that are now housed under its flag. Those blockbusters churned out for the mass market, with their computerised prose, as well as the various fiction vehicles spawned to make propaganda for some ideology or other, are not merely different in quality from the novels I am speaking of, but different in kind.

William Faulkner, in the famous interview originally published in *Paris Review* in 1956, was asked what he thought of his contemporaries. His reply is of some relevance to the theme I'm pursuing. It would seem at first to call it into question; but fundamentally, I think it confirms it.

> All of us failed to match our dreams of perfection. So I rate us on the basis of our splendid failure to do the impossible . . .
>
> I am a failed poet. Maybe every novelist tries to write poetry first, finds he can't and then tries the short story, which is the most demanding form after poetry, and failing that only then does he take up novel writing . . .

I don't know how far Faulkner had his tongue into his cheek when making this reply; I suspect half way. But if you take his statement perfectly literally, it's both ironic and illuminating. Ironic, since Faulkner is not just a major novelist but one of the great narrative poets of the century, and since novels such as *Light in August*, *The Wild Palms* and *The Sound and the Fury* are among those works which actually helped to bring into being the new kind of novel I am discussing – containing as they do passage after passage which, removed from context and printed as prose poems, would make the reputation of any minor poet – while the works in their totality are equalled only by the greatest verse collections of the period. The statement is also illuminating in that it probably reveals the sense of inferiority under which even Faulkner had to labour because of the long-standing notion of the 'impurity' of the novel, and its natural inferiority to verse: the idea that the novel could not finally be a poetic form; and that prose is base metal to poetry's gold.

This is a form of snobbery which dies hard – especially among some verse writers. Before contending with it, however, one has to allow that they are right in one thing: no half-way house can be built between verse and the novel. That's like the alchemists' attempt to turn base metal into gold: always doomed to failure, since the novel which attempts to absorb all the methods of verse ends by being minor and pretentious: neither good verse nor good prose. This was the case even with Hermann Broch's *The Death of Virgil*, one of the most monumental and interesting attempts yet made to marry the two forms. Its excursions into verse are laboured, refusing to leave the ground, and merely sound jarring beside the prose passages. But accurate though this contention of the exclusivist verse writer is, it fails to recognise that true poetic prose is not only a different discipline from the prose of the newspaper report or the commercial blockbuster, but from verse as well. Heightened prose isn't a poor man's poetry, but a different form of poetry, with its own technical demands, its own particular cadences. It isn't flowery or overblown; it's often quite spare, since prose must always say what it has to as directly as possible. Its test is in the way it reads aloud; and you need to have an ear to hear it. There's a typical and archetypal sound to such prose. We can hear it in the book of Ecclesiastes, in the King James Bible; in *A Christmas Carol*; in *Alice in Wonderland*; in *The Tailor of Gloucester*; in *Youth*; in *A Passage to India*; in *Death in Venice*; in *Light in August*; in *The Great Gatsby*; in *The Alexandria Quartet*.

But sound is only part of it. The aims of the novels and short stories I'm talking about are also essentially poetic – in the essential, not the superficial sense of that term. Such works tend to do two things at once: they tell a story, and they work through extended metaphors – which are not decorations, but organic to the narrative itself, and which set up echoes, like the multiple themes in a symphony. This is why their endings in particular are symphonic, and can move people so deeply, as the last passages do in *Gatsby*, or in James Joyce's *The Dead*. Isolated, these passages would simply be pieces of 'fine writing'; but in the poetic novel or short story, they are much more than that, having been prepared for all along. The primary and secondary themes have all been worked out, and the revelation now is both emotional and intellectual: everything has been confirmed, with shattering effect. This is what makes the death of von Aschenbach, at the end of *Death in Venice*, so tragically satisfying; and it's what makes the final paragraph of James Joyce's *The Dead* one of the most beautiful passages of poetic prose ever written. This attention to structure and metaphor, if one wants to be stringent about it, means that poetic fiction is not merely classifiable by cadence or by richness of writing, but by internal method. It means that D. H. Lawrence, for example, though indisputably a superb poet in prose, is not in this aspect a poetic novelist; whereas E. M. Forster, with his Jane Austenish dryness and deceptive simplicity, and Thomas Mann, with his vast, fastidious control and intellectual care, are two of the very greatest. Works of poetic fiction end by saying what cannot be said through direct statement, or even through inference. This was what Wolfe, Fitzgerald and Faulkner were all attempting; and Faulkner clearly had his two contemporaries in mind when he made his *Paris Review* statement. It is the nature of the poetic novel, as well as of all real poetry, to attempt to express the impossible and never quite to achieve it. Were it ever fully achieved, there would be no further need to write, as Faulkner himself recognised in an earlier part of the *Paris Review* statement:

> In my opinion if I could write all my work again I would do it better, which is the healthiest condition for the artist . . . that's why he keeps on working, trying again – he believes each time he will bring it off.

The three Americans have as their literary cousins Joseph Conrad, Virginia Woolf, Joyce and Proust; and in ways that are not so obvious they have an ancestor in Dickens – in whose works places and objects assume the terrible, dreamlike intensity characteristic of poetic fiction, and where certain motifs and even characters have a function that is more symbolic than naturalistic. The debt to Conrad in particular was plainly acknowledged by Fitzgerald; and it is always clear in Faulkner, who brings a characteristic method and preoccupation of Conrad's to a new level: I mean the vivid arrest of time and motion, specifically dealt with by Conrad in the famous preface to *The Nigger of the Narcissus*:

> To arrest, for the space of a breath, the hands busy about the work of the earth, and compel men entranced by the sight of distant goals to glance for a moment at the surrounding

vision of form and colour, of sunshine and shadows; to make them pause for a look, for a sigh, for a smile – such is the aim, difficult and evanescent, and reserved only for a very few to achieve.

For Wolfe, and for Fitzgerald too, Time was the enemy, but also the source of the buried, unlivable life they yearned for, constantly bearing them backwards; but for Faulkner, as for Conrad, the need was also to freeze present time so that just for a moment, 'for the space of a breath', all was grasped, all was seen, the minute and the marvellous and the fearful made deathless and comprehensible forever. Faulkner's novels live for these timeless moments of pause; that hiatus only possible in art, when the flux is arrested: the electric halt of the Spanish flamenco dancer; the heartrending stillness of the figures on Keats's Grecian urn. In one of the most extraordinary of such moments in Faulkner's work, the helpless protagonists are the convict and the pregnant woman in the skiff, caught in the fury of the great Mississippi floods of 1927, in *The Wild Palms*:

And while the woman huddled in the bows, aware or not aware, the convict . . . continued to paddle directly into it. Again he simply had not had time to order his rhythm-hypnotized muscles to cease. He continued to paddle though the skiff had ceased to move forward at all but seemed to be hanging in space while the paddle still reached, thrust, recovered and reached again; now, instead of space, the skiff became abruptly surrounded by a welter of fleeing debris – planks, small buildings, the bodies of drowned yet antic animals, entire trees leaping and diving like porpoises above which the skiff seemed to hover in weightless and airy indecision like a bird above a fleeing country-side . . . while the convict squatted in it still going through the motions of paddling, waiting for an opportunity to scream.

With its brilliant, wildly comical arrest of terrific velocity, this is like a frozen frame in cinema – but with another whole dimension which only words can encompass. Long one of the chief preoccupations of poetry, that dimension has now been made the territory of the novelist, for whom the natural world, the life of objects, and altered perceptions have become as much his subjects as character and events.

## 3

These heights gained so recently for fiction are lately being taken advantage of by very few writers.

The works that draw most attention at present are witty, quasi-picaresque novels, or works whose sole purpose, despite their ventures into the surreal, is social comment; or documentaries disguised as novels, which neatly sidestep the supreme creative task of invention. It's to be hoped that this phase is temporary, since it represents a return to a more rudimentary stage of fiction.

Another dubious trend has been towards dehumanisation. As the 'serious' novel sees itself moving into the position verse has long had – no longer the major popular medium, but one for a supposedly cultivated minority – it is heading in some quarters towards experiment for its own sake: always the sign of a minor art form. That old clown surrealism has been run on stage again, and we have a trivialisation in which time sequences and commonly perceived reality are disarranged, and personality and character almost cease to exist. When I call this trivialisation, I'm sure I'll encounter disagreement; but I'd submit that there is usually really very little of conceptual substance under the absurdist surface; and worse, that it's fragmentary, easy writing. Faulkner achieved an effective dislocation of time in *The Sound and the Fury*; but his was a work in which the other essential elements of fiction were powerfully present. The same applies with Kafka's transformation of the normal into nightmare; but their contemporary descendants usually have neither their skills nor their vision. The creation of character and dramatic momentum surely remain the real, hard work of the novel; and a form which seeks not only to depict but to interpret the nature and flow of life can't let go of these things. If it does, it loses its way, and in the end, it loses its audience. I've always been impressed by a story about the T'ang poet Po Chü-I, one of the greatest poets in any literature, who is loved in China as no other poets except Tu Fu and Li Po are loved. He used to read his poems to an old washerwoman; and if she didn't understand them, he rewrote them until she did. This is the norm to which literature must constantly return.

I understand that Robbe-Grillet, who did much to set the current trend, has rationalised by saying in effect that since God isn't here any more, purpose is a myth, meaning is an illusion, and we are reduced to describing surfaces. Wardrobes; streets; doors; why not? Human beings have no great importance; the intellect and the moral sense are both of doubtful validity. The first premise seems to me questionable; but even if God has gone away, the conclusion that we should sulk and depict the world of the clinically insane seems something of a cop-out; and the search for worth and validity in human beings and human society would seem to be even more urgent.

Fortunately, the novel has greater resilience than this. And I don't share the low opinion that some writers seem to have of the intelligence of the average man and woman. Major art forms have major audiences, and there are thousands of non-literary people out there to whom a good novel still has instant and powerful appeal. But the novel's tie with shared reality must be maintained, or its meaning and importance for such people will wither. The tie can be very tenuous, and the line where common day is lost is a very fluid one. To take one example: the Nighttown scene in Joyce's *Ulysses* gains its power simply through being tied to a grotesque yet troubling reality – that reality all too well known to us where nightmare and dream and guilt bubble under the surface, and then invade. But when the rocks of reality and consistent personality are lost altogether, then why should we care, and why should we believe? We lose interest, we can't identify; it's a private game, a minor entertainment. A work of literature is a social act, and there's no such thing as no point of view in the novel. Nihilism, which is back with us again, is itself a point of view. It's a refusal to care; and the writer must care (not cunningly pretend to care), if he's to move us. Recently, I was expressing this view to a professor of literature in Peking, and he said triumphantly: 'Ah – then in this you agree with us!' For a moment, since I am no Marxist, I was startled; but then I realised he was right. We had in common a belief that fiction must affirm the central worth of human beings.

Whatever we all may think of the novel, there's plenty of evidence of its continuing vitality: in particular, in its relationship to its rival fiction form the film. I'm sometimes not sure how real the rivalry is: the two storytelling forms may well be complementary, feeding off each other. Novelists now use many of the cinema's narrative techniques; and it is noticeable that film and television keep rifling the novel for material, and often find their biggest audiences for their interpretations of the giants of the form: nearly all of whom wrote for sound, not just sense.

That special pleasure which we learned as children, listening to the sly and exquisite cadences of Beatrix Potter and Hans Andersen, is a private matter: something the visual medium can't provide. Film-making is a team sport, and as we all know, the writer is the one everyone kicks around, and terrible things are done to his screenplay. But teams, although they have a lot of fun, tend only to produce enchanting minor art. For the other sort of creation, there is no substitute for a lonely man or woman sitting in a room; and as any novelist will tell you, it involves unpicking all you've done again and again, and going back to weave it all again: not once, not twice, but maybe half a dozen times. It's a price few people want to pay, but the reward is what film directors call creative control. In the film world, everyone knows that's an illusion; but in the novel, it's real.

For that reason, I believe the novel will endure; and I will go on writing them. The novel as a simple tale well told might as well stand aside for the film, and the excellent TV dramas now appearing; but what will remain, I think, are the sorts of novel I've been speaking of. These novels may be wanted more, not less. They can't achieve the magical vividness, the total illusion of the film. But what they can do is to present us with the whole landscape of experience; the full nature of the soul's journey. And now, more than ever, we need to encounter those voices that are heard in silence. Without them, we may lose a part of ourselves.

# Notes

CROSSING THE GAP

11 'These things I knew about': Nor Hall, *The Moon and the Virgin*,
London: The Women's Press, 1980.

15 'In the cult . . .': Nirad Chaudhuri, *The Continent of Circe*, London:
Chatto & Windus, 1965.

16 'Sanskrit': from the cycle 'Walking to the Cattle Place' in Les
Murray, *The Vernacular Republic*, Sydney: Angus & Robertson, 1982.

CALIFORNIA DREAMING, HERMANN HESSE AND
THE GREAT GOD POT

60 Charlie Manson: for the full account of the Manson family
murders and Charles Manson's ideas, I am indebted to Prosecutor
Vincent Bugliosi and Curt Gentry, *Helter Skelter*, London: The
Bodley Head, 1975.

61 'a psychedelic journey': Timothy Leary and Ralph Metzner,
'Hermann Hesse: Poet of the Interior Journey', *Psychedelic Review*
1, 1963.

63 Ralph Freedman, *Hermann Hesse, Pilgrim of Crisis*, London:
Jonathan Cape, 1979.

68 Satanists: see Bugliosi and Gentry, *Helter Skelter*.

THE LAST NOVELIST

71 Matthew J. Bruccoli, *Some Sort of Epic Grandeur: The Life of F. Scott
Fitzgerald*, London: Hodder & Stoughton, 1981.

75 Matthew J. Bruccoli, *Scott and Ernest – The Authority of Failure and
the Authority of Success*, London: The Bodley Head, 1978.

THE LOST HEMISPHERE

96 Les Murray, 'The Returnees', in *The Vernacular Republic*.

97 Albert Camus, 'Summer in Algiers', in *Myth of Sisyphus*, translated
by J. O'Brien, London: Hamish Hamilton, 1955.

98 'While children fret': Geoffrey Lehmann, 'Aqueducts', in *Nero's
Poems*, Sydney: Angus & Robertson, 1981.

99 'There's sand': Geoffrey Lehmann, 'By the Sea', in *Nero's Poems*.

99 Geoffrey Lehmann, 'Night Flower', in *A Voyage of Lions*, Sydney: Angus & Robertson, 1968.

100 'I'll pass a law': Geoffrey Lehmann, 'Potters' Field', in *Nero's Poems*.

100 'There is another meaning': Vivian Smith, 'The Other Meaning', in *Tide Country*, Sydney: Angus & Robertson, 1982.

101 'They'll not find him': Vivian Smith, 'Thylacine', in *Tide Country*.

101 'In here is like . . .': Les Murray, 'The Gum Forest', in *The Vernacular Republic*.

A TASMANIAN TONE

107 *Jail Journal* by John Mitchel, Prisoner in the hands of the English, Dublin: M. H. Gill & Son, Ltd, 1854.

108 'In vain I try . . .': *Jail Journal*.

109 'I came down . . .': Vivian Smith, 'Bird Sanctuary', in *Tide Country*.

110 'Water colour country': Vivian Smith, 'Tasmania', in *Tide Country*.

110 'Someone said': Vivian Smith, 'Fishermen, Drowned Beyond the West Coast', in *Tide Country*.

111 'colonial shipping': I am quoting from 'An Excursion to Port Arthur in 1842' by David Burn, published in the *Tasmanian Journal* of that year.

114 'better than where they were': Report of a Select Committee, 1838. 'Two or three men murdered their fellow prisoners . . . apparently without malice . . . stating that they knew they should be hanged, but it was better than being where they were.'

115 James McQueen, 'Night Run', in *The Electric Beach*, Wynyard, Tasmania: Robin Books, 1978.

115 Hal Porter, *The Tilted Cross*, London: Faber & Faber, 1961.

116 'On one of these . . .': James McQueen, *Hook's Mountain*, Melbourne: Macmillan Co. of Australia Ltd, 1982.

117 'A dark-green gum': James McAuley, 'St John's Park, Newtown', in *Collected Poems 1936–1970*, Sydney: Angus & Robertson, 1971.

118 'Ocean, heaven': Gwen Harwood, 'Oyster Cove Pastorals, 2: High Noon', in *The Lion's Bride*, Sydney: Angus & Robertson, 1981.

MYSTERIES

119 'Go out and camp': Roland Robinson, 'Mapooram', in *Altjeringa*, Sydney: A. W. & A. H. Reed [date unknown].

121 For a fuller report of the Taylor case, see the *Daily Mail* (London) of 23 April 1975 and *Time* magazine of 5 May 1975.

123 Neville Drury and Gregory Tillett, *Other Temples, Other Gods: The Occult in Australia*, Lane Cove: Hodder & Stoughton (Australia) Ltd, 1982.

124 Cut Throat: see the report in *The Sun* (Sydney), 7 February 1986.

125 Colin Wilson, *Mysteries*, London: Hodder & Stoughton, 1979.

129 Frédéric Ozanam, *A History of Civilization in the Fifth Century*, London, 1868.

136 'Though it makes no great gesture': Baudelaire, 'Préface', in *Les Fleurs du Mal*.

136 'He signalled me': Carlos Castaneda, *Journey to Ixtlán*, London: The Bodley Head, 1973.

137 'Genaro is going': Carlos Castaneda, *Journey to Ixtlán*.

138 'I saw instantly': Carlos Castaneda, *Tales of Power*, London: Hodder & Stoughton, 1975.

138 'The antidote': Carlos Castaneda, *Tales of Power*.

139 'That dog's barking': Carlos Castaneda, *Tales of Power*.

140 'My parish': Georges Bernanos, *The Diary of a Country Priest*, London: Macmillan & Co., 1937.

THE NOVEL AS NARRATIVE POEM

144 'Remembering speechlessly': Thomas Wolfe, *Look Homeward, Angel*, New York: Charles Scribner's Sons, 1929.

145 'Trains cross the continent': Thomas Wolfe, *Of Time and the River*, New York: Charles Scribner's Sons, 1935.

147 strip cartoons: Pat Sullivan, Australian-born, was the creator of 'Felix the Cat'; Lee Falk drew 'The Phantom'; Jim Bancks was the creator of 'Ginger Meggs'; and Kate O'Brien created 'Wanda the War Girl'. These last two were Australian strips, at the peak of their popularity in the 1940s.

151 'This garden': Kenneth Slessor, 'Pan at Lane Cove', in *Poems*, Sydney: Angus & Robertson, 1944.

153 Vincent Buckley, 'In the Shadow of Patrick White', *Meanjin Quarterly*, no. 2, 1961.

160 'And while the woman': William Faulkner, 'Old Man', from *The Wild Palms*, Harmondsworth, Middlesex: Penguin Books, 1970.